Are We Driving up the Right Riverbed?

David Collison

SOCCIONES

S☀CCIONES

© David Collison 2017

All rights reserved

ISBN-13: 978-1978211032
ISBN-10: 1978211031

Cover design © Socciones

Design & formatting by Socciones Editoria Digitale
www.kindle-publishing-service.co.uk

This book is dedicated to our friends Tony and Monique, Martin and Denise, Roger and Pepe who helped us along the way.

CONTENTS

PART ONE

LOS TABLONES

CHAPTER ONE
First Viewing

It was 4.00 p.m. one afternoon in November 1988. We were staying in a friend's country cottage in the foothills of the Sierra Nevada mountains a few miles from the city of Motril on the south coast of Spain. My girlfriend, Alison, was snoozing contentedly in the Andalucian sunshine - a collapsible food cover made of netting perched on her face to ward off the flies - when I rushed up with the good news.

"I have just been talking to that nice Dutch couple we met the other day and apparently there is a ruined cottage for sale not five minutes from here, and it's going really cheap!"

The information did not elicit the enthusiastic response anticipated. Why the quizzical look? After all, we *had* spent the previous two weeks wandering around the hills, discovering abandoned ruins and fantasizing about which one would make the best holiday hideaway.

"Karel has offered to show it to us. Now. Are you coming?"

"I am not sure it is such a good idea," she replied, "we don't speak Spanish. We probably can't afford it. And anyway, we are going home tomorrow."

This negative attitude was so out of character that, for a moment, I was taken completely off guard. Then she continued, "It might be a bit soon to think of buying a house together, don't you think?"

The penny dropped. In my usual unthinking enthusiasm for a new project, I was overlooking the fact that we had only known each other for a year or so, during which time, because of our careers, we had spent little serious time together. It was hardly surprising she had reservations about purchasing a house in a foreign land with someone she did not know that well and with whom a long-term relationship had never been discussed.

"It's only looking at a ruin," I said. "We don't have to take it any further."

"Oh, all right," she replied, reluctantly stirring from the comfortable lounger. And we set off on what I secretly hoped would turn out to be a great adventure.

The Dutchman who was going to show us the ruin was staying with his wife, Eva, in a house owned by our friends Roger and his partner. Expecting to find Roger at home, we paid a call and discovered that Karel and Eva were looking after the house while Roger and his partner were away for a few weeks. Invited in for a coffee, we found them totally charming and very knowledgeable about this area of the south coast of Spain. Rather annoyingly, they spoke fluent Spanish, fluent English and goodness knows how many other languages apart from their native Dutch.

Now, Karel, early forties, soft-spoken and slightly gangly, was waiting for us on the narrow tarmac road that led away from the nearby tiny village of Los Tablones. Together we headed up a dusty track and after a quarter of a mile Karel stopped and pointed.

"That is your ruin. See? Just beyond the white house on the right. At the weekends people live in that house. I have talked to the man. They are good neighbours."

Perched precariously on the top of a steep ravine (or *barranco)*, the little building looked in a sorry state. An estate agent might have described it as having great potential for improvement.

On the other hand, the traditional mud and stone walls seemed solid enough and the tiled roof was in reasonable repair, as was the large beehive-like structure attached to one end of the house - a bread oven.

Walking round to the front of the L-shaped building, we were immediately captivated by the glorious view. In the distance rose a magnificent range of mountains, the Sierra Nevada. A river could be seen far below running along the bottom of the *barranco* on the far side of which Alison pointed out a goatherd with some fifty or sixty goats scampering up and down between the olive trees. Also on the far side of the valley was what looked like a very long stone wall. Karel explained that this was a Roman aqueduct built for irrigation purposes when wheat was grown on the terraced hillsides. Also on the far side of the valley was what looked like a very long stone wall. Karel explained that this was a Roman aqueduct built for irrigation purposes when wheat was grown on the terraced hillsides. To the far left could be seen an enormous circular structure, possible a reservoir, also built by the Romans. A subsequent exploration of the site revealed two remarkably smooth cylindrical shafts, about a metre in diameter, set into the top of the thick wall on the near side of the edifice. They ran vertically down to emerge in the valley far below. We imagined that this was all part of the ancient irrigation system but Roger had another theory. He maintained that this was where grain, threshed on a flat stone floor on the hillside above, was stored waiting to be poured down the shafts and loaded onto carts for transport to the town.

For four hundred years, from around 20 BC, Andalucia was one of Rome's richest and best-organized colonies. The fact that the grain tower and aqueduct remained virtually intact after all those centuries was remarkable.

On our side of the valley the ground was fairly flat with more olive trees stretching away into the distance. Exactly the same view would have been experienced by generations of people making a meager living in this area by harvesting olives and tending their goats. Everywhere the ground was covered with clumps of wild thyme pervading the atmosphere with an evocative sweet scent.

Roman structure

5

Karel explained that he and Eva had seriously considered buying this little house, or *cortijo* (pronounced 'cort<u>ee</u>ho') but had eventually decided against it.

"The *cortijo* is perfect, but we need to grow fruit and vegetables. To live as self-sufficient. That is important for us. There is much land but it is too rocky, too hard for planting. But for you this is not a problem."

"What exactly do you mean by *much* land"?

Karel indicated a carob tree some two hundred yards away on the strip of flat ground in front of the house and said that the boundary to the south was just beyond that. At the rear of the house to the north the land extended for about half that distance.

"Do you mean to say that we would own all of this land along here beside the track?"

"Oh no. Much more. The track running beside the house is the east boundary. The west boundary is right down to the river. The whole of the hillside."

The whole of the hillside! It must be several acres. Mostly almost vertical, of course, but to actually own a hillside - or a large part of a hillside - in Spain!

Alison brought me back to reality by suggesting that we should look inside the building and see what sort of state it was in.

Pushing open the rickety front door, Karel led us into the largest of three rooms comprising the living area of the house. This rectangular space measuring 16' 6" x 10' 6" (5m x 3.2m) had an attractive sloping ceiling supported by round beams (thin tree trunks) running from the highest point at the far wall down to about five foot six (1.3m). Between the roof beams and the tiles was a layer of reeds *(cañavera)*. All this plus the top section of the walls was painted with an unfortunate shade of baby-poo yellow. The rest of the room was painted white, much of which had cracked off with flakes scattering the floor amongst an assortment of old bottles, tin cans, bits of wood and sacking. Most of the original clay floor tiles had been pilfered leaving just bare earth. Strangely, there was no window in the room and when the front door was closed it became unpleasantly gloomy.

In the far wall to the left of the entrance was a fireplace *(chiminea)* with a shelf running the width of the room at high level around the chimney breast. A lower shelf extended to the right of the mantle piece and below this was a surface that looked like a seat. To the left of the fireplace, was a solid construction creating a surface at waist height.

We had seen similar *chimineas* in the other ruins we had explored. Obviously designed for a purpose, we had not been able to work out exactly what this was. Karel came to the rescue, explaining that what we were looking at was a sophisticated cooking range.

At the heart of the whole thing was the fireplace that had an opening half way up the back wall providing access to the bread oven. Originally, there would have been some kind of door or panel to retain the heat once a fire had been lit inside the oven. Being an enclosed space, the oven would rapidly become hot enough for inserting the bread dough. Regularly used for baking bread, the oven would also have been used to cook other foods and was spacious enough to roast a goat.

Karl pointed out the solid section to the left of the fireplace. At present it was covered with many layers of white paint, but if this were to be removed, clay tiles covering the top surface would be revealed and, just below the tiles in the front face, there should be two holes. Looking for all the world like bottle racks, we had noticed these holes in other *cortijos*. We were now to learn how these "bottle racks" had an important function. They were designed to take burning wood from the fireplace in order to heat up the clay tiles. The tile above one of the recesses acted as a hot plate while the tile above the other recess had a hole in it to accommodate a round-bottomed clay cooking pot. The whole thing was a simple but effective cooking hob. Mystery solved.

Another feature seen in every *cortijo* was an arched recess, usually in the wall opposite the door, as was the case here. It had two shelves, probably for displaying personal possessions and religious devotions, below which was a solid base with two large indentations designed to hold round-bottomed jars for water or olive oil. Water had to be collected from the nearest stream that, in this case, involved a very long scramble down the *barranco* and an exhausting climb back up. Built into the corner of the room beside the recess were the remains of a large pottery jar, presumably to be filled with water.

To the right of the *chiminea*, a low archway led into the second room. It was about a third the size of the main room and seemed in a better state. The walls were painted white and there was a small window. We were delighted to see an old Spanish bed frame in reasonable repair and there was also a battered but interesting looking chest, another traditional feature.

Although the accommodation was - one had to admit - modest, it had a wonderfully cosy atmosphere and I was imagining what it would be like with clean white walls, terracotta tiled floors, a few choice pieces of rustic furniture and, maybe, a colourful rug or two. Alison, meanwhile, thinking along more practical lines, wanted to know how one could possibly fit in a few essentials such as a kitchen, a bathroom and a lavatory.

With a knowing smile, Karel ushered us back into the main room. Through a low arched opening in the wall to the right of the front door was a third room. All the doors and archways were only 5'00" to 5' 6" (1.5m to 1.7m) high; perfectly adequate for the peasant population of the past. And for Alison.

Because the house was built on a slope, there were two steps down into this room. Consequently, the ceiling was quite high. The airy rectangular space was the same width as the main room; perfect for turning into a kitchen.

OK so far, but what about a bathroom?

Once again our Dutch friend had a plan. He beckoned us and we followed him out of the front door and down the slope to a shed door in an extension to the building. He explained that this had probably been a stable for a donkey but vestiges of shriveled olives and blackened almonds on the dirt floor, plus some broken timber racks indicated that it had latterly been used as a store. With a grand gesture, Karel indicated the area that measured about 6' 6" (2m) square.

"And here is your bathroom."

I was immediately enthused and could visualise the layout with a washbasin, shower, toilet and even a small bath. The floor was considerably lower than the main house, but it would be possible to build some steps and knock a doorway through to the kitchen.

Alison, on the other hand, was more concerned with another practical problem: the *cortijo* had no water. There was no mains water supply in the hills, so we would have to build a large water tank similar to the one at our friend's house. This had to be filled when necessary by ordering a tanker from the nearby town of Motril.

It was obvious that Alison and I both loved the place and could see the possibilities, but she was becoming increasingly concerned about the amount of work involved and the investment. And what about electricity? There was a rather dodgy looking electric cable coming to a metal pole fixed to the side of the building, so presumably a supply was available, but there were no lights, no plug sockets and no meter. More expense. And we had yet to discover the actual price of the house. What exactly *was* "very cheap"?

Karel said that a meeting could be arranged with Paco, the owner, to discuss the price. Even if we decided against it, nothing would be lost. The main problem was lack of time. We were leaving for England the following afternoon, so Karel suggested a meeting that evening at Paco's bar/restaurant in Motril. This was agreed and Karel headed off to make the arrangements.

Back at the house, I was enthusing about the project, but I could see that Alison still had enormous reservations, even suggesting that we should cancel this evening's meeting. With some trepidation, I brought up the subject of our relationship and it turned out that she imagined the next step in our relationship, far from buying a ruin in Spain, would be a suggestion from me that she might like to leave a toothbrush at my place.

Now that the subject had been broached, it dawned on me with a sickening thud that she, quite reasonably, might not see herself permanently tied to a 51-year old divorcee with three children who, let's face it, was a

9

tad more than twenty years her senior. All things considered, perhaps not the best catch.

For the first time, I explained my feelings and my assumption - perhaps unfounded - that we were both it for the long term. For my part, because we seemed such a natural pair and life was interesting and full of fun, I just imagined that we would be together and everything would be lovely.

To my great relief, she smiled, saying, "Well, there is no harm in going to see what the man has to say, I suppose."

Agreeing that we should continue to investigate the possibility of buying a ruin in the Spanish hills, I took to be an important commitment in more ways than one.

So here we were, on the day before we flew back to England, without a word of Spanish between us, contemplating the purchase of a property with some unknown Spaniard in a bar in Motril. What could possibly go wrong? It was just a matter of waiting until 7.00 p.m. and our rendezvous at Paco's Bar.

Alison and the arched recess opposite the front door

Bedroom

Kitchen

Karel and Alison outside the donkey house

CHAPTER TWO
Meeting a Princess

Cash was probably going to be the deciding factor. Following my divorce, it was mutually agreed that the family home should remain with my three children and their mother. Left with limited resources, I had purchased a small houseboat on Taggs Island near Hampton Court. From there, it was not too difficult to get up to my workplace in London's Covent Garden. I was a director of the Theatre Projects group, originally concerned with the design and supply of lighting and sound equipment, we were now involved with the production of West End plays and musicals and had a company providing a consultancy service for new theatre buildings. My area of expertise was in sound, and during the 1970s and 80s I had devised sound systems for many original West End shows such as "Fiddler on the Roof", "Company", "Cabaret" and "Jesus Christ Superstar", but now I was more involved with management.

One of my long-term clients, for whom we created sound effects in our recording studio, was Richard Gill, founder of the very successful Polka Children's Theatre in Wimbledon, and it was he who indirectly brought Alison and me together.

I had designed the sound for a musical production in Denmark of Hans Andersen's fairy tale "The Tinder Box". This was in a delightful little theatre in the town of Aalborg. I was so struck with the show that I wrote an English version of the story omitting the songs. I had noticed that the children, totally involved in the narrative, tended to loose interest as soon as anyone started singing. Without any great expectations, I showed the script to Richard Gill and, to my surprise, he said that he would like to put it on. To my even greater surprise, he suggested that I should direct it. This was a new departure for me, but I thought "Why not?" and arranged for my annual holiday to coincide with the scheduled rehearsal period.

The story, as you might know, is all about a poor soldier, a quest for treasure involving encounters with dogs with eyes as big as saucers, eyes as big as dinner plates, and eyes as big as millstones. And, of course, there is a beautiful princess. You can imagine how the story eventually leads to a happy ending.

I had written the part of the Princess as a feisty young girl who had tantrums and argued a lot with her long suffering parents – not your usual run-of-the-mill fairytale princess - and one of the actresses auditioning really entered into the character, shouting, grimacing and jumping up and down with rage. It was very funny, just as I had hoped, and I determined to give her the part. The decision, you have to believe, was in no way swayed by the fact that during the audition she innocently enquired from the stage:

"Who wrote this script? It really is very good."

I discovered later that Alison had worked at Polka Theatre several times before and it was entirely possible that someone had told her who was the author – a possibility she has always stoutly denied.

Rehearsals were fun and, judging by the reaction of the children, the show was a success. Towards the end of the four-week run, I plucked up courage and asked Alison if she would care to accompany me to the first night of a West End play, explaining that it was a show produced by Theatre Projects. I was delighted when she accepted. Of course, her decision might have had something to do with the fact that, as an actress about to be out of work, making friends with someone involved with a West End production company could be a smart move.

What she did not know was that our group of companies was in serious financial trouble, largely because, during an ambitious programme of expansion, bank loans had soared to an unsustainable 20%. All but the very successful consultancy company was being sold off and within a year I was to change careers and set up my own company designing historically based visitor attractions. That is another story, but hence my lack of funds.

At the end of our first date, we agreed to meet again and exchanged telephone numbers. However, the relationship could well have ended at this point. By error, the number I gave her was wrong. This she discovered when ringing to thank me for the evening, concluding that this might have been a deliberate ploy to prevent further contact. Not being one to give up that easily, she worked her way through permutations of the number until she eventually got through to me. During the conversation, she expressed interest in my houseboat and I suggested that she might like to visit the following weekend. However, the offer was declined. There was some excuse about a younger brother arriving home from a year-long trip to Australia. A likely tale, I thought. Fortunately, the following week I plucked up courage and gave it one more go. This time she accepted.

As much time as possible was spent together during the following weeks, although opportunities were limited. Involved with crisis management of our group of companies, I was having to work long days. This usually meant Alison driving from her flat near Woolwich to the houseboat on Taggs Island, a journey of up to an hour and a half. So when my very good friend Tony Horder offered us his house in Spain for a holiday, we jumped at the opportunity.

Tony and I had worked together in the recording studio creating sound effects for theatres up and down the country for many years and later, when I began to work on musicals as a sound designer, he joined me in this new enterprise. There were no other sound designers in the theatre at the time, so we happily made up the rules as we went along. The object in those days was to make the performers heard above the orchestra while retaining the natural sound of the human voice. The audience should not be aware of microphones - which was a good trick if you could pull it off. This was some years before radio systems were developed so that every performer in a musical could wear a personal microphone. The public now seems to accept a louder than life electronic sound.

Aside from creating sound effects and working on the occasional musical, Tony became involved with fashion shows, organizing all the recorded music and, sometimes, even acting as compère. Through this involvement with the fashion industry, he met two people who were to change his life. Firstly, he became friendly with a very attractive French lady who worked in the Paris office of Courtaulds, the giant clothing manufacturer, and their friendship blossomed until he and Monique eventually decided to marry. Sadly for me, this meant Tony saying farewell to Britain for a new life in France.

The second person he befriended in the fashion world, named Roger, was a renowned designer and producer of fashion shows. Life in that business can be very stressful and when Roger had a cancer scare his doctor warned him that he should slow down. Taking this advice to heart, he promptly upped sticks and moved to the sunshine of Andalucia in southern Spain. In the middle of nowhere, near a small cluster of dwellings known as Los Tablones, he found a house with a piece of land large enough for his plan to grow sub tropical trees and plants. Later, he purchased two adjacent houses, all three in need of renovation.

His intention was to make the main house habitable for himself and partner, build a swimming pool, create an attractive garden, and then renovate the two other houses for holiday lets. Of course, being a designer, each of the buildings ended up looking like something out of "Homes and Gardens" Spanish style. It was fortuitous that Roger's partner, Robert (pronounced '*Robair*' because he had French and Spanish parents) had building skills, but it soon became obvious that Roger himself was no slouch when it came to cement and brickwork.

Once they had one of the rental houses in a fit state, Tony was invited to stay. He was immediately smitten by the views of hills and mountains, the peaceful atmosphere and, of course, the sunshine. Then came the bombshell: Roger said that he had picked out a *cortijo* less than a quarter of a mile away and Tony simply *had* to buy it. Quite a bit of work needed doing, but nothing Tony could not handle.

So began a project involving Tony and Monique in many exhausting 24 hour drives from Paris to spend a few days or a couple of weeks building, renovating, repairing and decorating.

A mere four years later, Alison and I were able to enjoy the fruits of their labour when we had our first holiday together in their splendidly restored cottage.

CHAPTER THREE
How We Got There

Tony's instructions to find his house in Los Tablones proved a little less than adequate. After collecting the little hire car at Malaga airport, we drove westward along the coast road for some one and a half hours, passing through a few small towns and villages until we reached the larger town of Motril.

The landscape mainly consisted of rocky hillsides covered with scrub and olive trees, dotted with single story cottages. Some of these had whitewashed walls with orange roof tiles, but the majority were ruins in various states of decay. Occasionally, where the ground flattened out there were fields of crops, and we were surprised to see one of these fields being ploughed with a pair of oxen. To our right, throughout the entire journey there were views of the deep blue Mediterranean stretching away to the horizon.

Finding the road out of Motril towards Los Tablones proved a little more tricky, but that was before we hit the real problems. Once we had located the road, Tony had told us to turn left at a small group of houses just after a bridge. No details of mileage had been given and we passed several groups of houses before deciding that we must have missed the bridge. Retracing our steps, we noticed that the road passed over a small dried up stream and decided that this little hump in the road must be the bridge. Performing a U-turn, we began to look out for the turning "to be found just after a house with lush vegetation". Having just arrived from a particularly verdant Spring in England, nothing in this dry arid landscape appeared particularly "lush". However, after a while there was a house with some bougainvillea growing along the fence. Could this be it? Just beyond and to the left was indeed a narrow track, so that was the route we decided to take.

The next landmark on our list of instructions was a "round goat pound in front of a cottage". We were to knock on the door and ask for Maria, the goatherd's wife, who had the keys to Tony's house. There were no telephones anywhere near Los Tablones (this was long before mobile phones) so she was not expecting us. We were told to say: *Amigos de Tony. Llaves de la casa, por favor?* (Tony's friends. Keys for the house please?). Whether or not she would feel obliged to hand over the keys to two total strangers remained to be seen, there being no possibility of further explanation or discussion on either side.

17

After driving cautiously for some while on a track that snaked around the hills with sheer drops to one side or the other, we began to wonder if we had missed this goat pound or were quite possibly on the wrong road. Then Alison spied a house with a circular concrete construction beside it. That could be it. (We later discovered that these big round things, seen everywhere, were water tanks for irrigation). The door was opened by a cross-looking man, far too smartly-dressed to be a goatherd. He was chewing something, obviously disturbed from his mid-day meal. Nevertheless, with what I hoped was an engaging smile, I enquired:

"Maria?"

He eyed me with suspicion.

"Maria! No."

Not knowing how to continue the conversation, I tried the magic words:

"Amigos de Tony. Llaves de la casa, por favor?"

The man, who had no idea what these idiots were on about, spoke a few rapid sentences in Spanish, possibly trying to be helpful. More probably not. He then glared at us expectantly, obviously waiting for a response. Having pretty well exhausted our vocabulary, I ventured:

"Los Tablones?"

This he seemed to understand and immediately became voluble on the subject. Each time Los Tablones was mentioned, he cast his eyes heavenwards and gestured down the road. We were not sure whether he was giving us directions or warning us to steer clear of some kind of hell where the inhabitants were all mad and ate their children. We assumed, however, that we were heading in the right direction, so both muttering *si, gracias* and *adios* (our three other words) we made an undignified exit. When safely back in the car, to lighten the atmosphere that was growing ever more tense, I remarked:

"I thought we handled that well."

Alison gave me a withering look. To tell the truth, senses of humour were wearing thin all round. Conversation turned towards the possibility of abandoning the quest and returning to Motril to find a hotel. At least, Alison pointed out, they would have a telephone and we could contact Tony in Paris. I

18

thought it unwise at this particular juncture to admit that I had not thought to make a note of his number.

We motored on for another five minutes or so and came to a fork in the road. Which way to go? The roads ran either side of a little whitewashed house in front of which was a triangle of scrubby earth with a small tree and a tin water trough. Alison had a desperate thought:

"Do you think this could be the place?"

"Well, it is hardly a circular goat pound, is it? Surely a goat pound would have some sort of fence or wall and surely it would be circular... and there ought to be goats."

"For goodness sake, let's at least give it a try!"

"OK. OK."

So we knocked on the door and it was opened by a woman wearing a grey apron over a long shapeless black dress below which there was a glimpse of thick black stockings and well-worn slippers. She peered at us enquiringly.

"Maria?"

"Si."

Success! I was so surprised that I quite forgot my next line. Fortunately, Alison, being an actress, had a firmer grasp of the script and quickly interjected with the correct words. Because of our horrendous accents, the woman took a few moments to translate what was being said; but we must have appeared trustworthy souls because, after only a brief hesitation, she disappeared into the house to return a few moments later with the keys. There followed a piece of mime along the lines of "We have no idea where the wretched house is". Fortunately, she soon cottoned on and accompanied by many pointing and shooing motions, indicated a long white cottage just beyond a small rise. Taking leave of Maria with a chorus of *Graciases* and *Adioses*, we finally arrived at Tony's house, completely frazzled, but mightily relieved to have succeeded.

There followed ten days of sunshine, relaxation, and exploration of the local countryside. Much time was spent sampling the local wines, fruits and cheeses and eating deliciously fresh fish. In those days, long before the advent of the

EU and the euro, one could get an extremely good two-course meal in a restaurant with a glass of wine for 600 pesetas, less than £3.00 a head. Unfortunately, I became violently sick after one meal in a restaurant and we learned to avoid anything uncooked. Salads, for example, could have been washed in water from some unknown source.

Very few people, even in the big town of Motril, spoke a word of English, but that did not seem to matter. Everything was a huge adventure and we came across some extraordinary local characters, not least was Maria's husband, the goatherd. The reason that no goats were in evidence when we first arrived was because, at nights, they were all crammed into a large shed beside the house. Every morning, however, the "circular goat pound" became a seething mass of animals all waiting for Maria's husband to take them along the road and up into the hills to forage for food. This stocky figure striding along, grey shirt, black baggy trousers, black boots and black cap became a familiar sight. Trotting along by his side, attached to a rope was the lead goat with a bell around its neck making a constant tinkling sound. A black and white collie, barking excitedly, scampered around to head off any strays and the herd of sixty or seventy goats, their small hooves click-clacking on the tarmac, followed along, all happily jostling and loudly farting.

We were also fascinated by the wizened little man who trundled past each day with a large plastic bucket in a wheelbarrow. When he returned some time later, the bucket would be filled with water from a stream situated in the valley some long way down the road. Then there was the woman, known locally as *La Loca* (the mad woman), who actually lived in a kind of nest she had created in some bushes down by the stream. Tall and erect, she could often be seen striding across the hills. Years later, we discovered that she had once been a ballet dancer in France who, when suffering from some form of mental breakdown, was incarcerated in a series of institutions. Each time this happened, she had to escape because her symptoms included acute claustrophobia. Eventually the authorities lost patience and, according to the story she told a Spanish-speaking friend of ours, they simply popped her over the border into Spain. Determined to make her home in a warmer climate, she trudged south until finally stumbling upon Los Tablones.

We were enchanted by the huge covered market in Motril selling deliciously fresh fruit and vegetables and all kinds of exotic fish; the flat land around Motril with acres of orchards growing avocados, mangos, bananas and custard apples; and the fact that every woman over the age of about fifty wore black from head to foot and walked around the city streets in slippers.

Wandering the hills around Los Tablones, we discovered intriguing traces of cave dwellers where the openings to the caverns had been walled up with windows and doors. Inside some of the larger caves, there were partitions to create rooms and one even had wires indicating an electricity supply. Evidently, some of these caves had only recently been abandoned.

One of the highlights was getting to know Tony's friend Roger. I had met him briefly when introduced by Tony in our recording studio a year or two back. I recalled a tall, well-built quietly spoken man whose face often lit up with a coquettish smile.

Forewarned that we would be staying in Tony's house, a visit was expected and we received a warm welcome. Following introductions and pleasantries, he invited us to view his 'estate' and, my, were we impressed! A group of three houses with terracotta tiled roofs and rough walls painted white in the local style, with window frames and chunky doors all in dark stained timber. The houses were set amongst an exotic collection of cacti, flowers and trees providing welcome areas of shade. At a short distance from the houses, there was an orchard producing oranges, lemons, mangos, bananas, almonds and olives.

It turned out that Roger lived almost opposite the famous goat pound and had a friendly, if not intimate relationship with his neighbours. Maria, her husband and their two teenage daughters lived a very basic lifestyle in their *cortijo* with no bathroom or toilet facilities and no means of transport except for a battered old motorbike. Roger, with genuine concern, had offered to build them a proper lavatory, but the proposal was refused. They were too proud to accept charity, especially from a foreigner, preferring to continue using the goat shed as a toilet.

Roger

In stark contrast, the three houses renovated by Roger and Robert had proper kitchens and bathrooms with beautifully tiled floors and walls, and running water from a big round concrete water tank (*deposito*). The water, apart from being pumped into the house, served the network of irrigation pipes for the trees and plants on the land, and also filled the large circular swimming pool.

The local electricity supply was only powerful enough to run lighting systems, and power failures were a frequent occurrence as more and more people overloaded the system with pumps and other appliances. Consequently, Calor gas was used for cooking.

Unfortunately, neither Roger nor Tony had installed gas water heating in their properties, relying entirely on solar panels. Tony had just one solitary panel on his roof and while it is true the sun blazes down most days, when we wanted to take a shower before retiring for the night, the system had cooled and the water was hardly warm. Tony later pointed out that there had been no hot water at all during most of the renovation work, so he had been excited to have free hot water during the day and anything above freezing during the hours of darkness was a bonus. Roger was soon forced to install gas water heaters following complaints from paying guests. Tony followed suit when funds became available.

As Roger proudly showed us round his houses, we were surprised to discover

Alison in one of Roger's houses

that many of the interesting pieces of furniture and unusual features had been purchased cheaply in junk shops or simply picked up from rubbish tips. He had a designer's eye for spying bits of discarded wood, old light fittings, pieces of metal, etc., that could be renovated and used to wonderful effect. For example, one of the houses had an old earthenware bath set into a wooden feed trough from a pony shed. With a tasteful tile surround and terracotta steps to enter the bath, it looked a million dollars.

The rooms all had beamed ceilings and between the beams were either *cañavera* (reeds), rustic tiles or white plaster. Hanging behind some of the beds were colourful carpets made in villages high up in the Alpujarras, only an hour or so away. A number of attractive paintings with the same signature caught our eye and we were surprised to be introduced to the artist. Roger's partner, Robert, not only possessed building skills but he was a sensitive and talented painter.

Relaxing in the garden under the shade of the trees, we chatted about Roger's former career in the fashion business and how, having found this little bit of heaven, he could never contemplate returning to that kind of existence.

"Look around. We have peace, we have vegetables springing up in the garden all year round, fruit dropping off the trees, cheap wine... and sunshine. What more could you want?"

What more indeed? The thought of returning to London and our pressured lives in the theatre was not very appealing, especially as I had to face battling with the problems of a company in serious financial difficulties. Whatever happened, we were determined to make another visit to Los Tablones as soon a possible, assuming that our good friends would once again be willing to lend us their house.

Fortunately, Tony and Monique were keen to have *El Cortijuelo* (the little farmhouse) used as much as possible and, a year later, we were to return - and that is when we became involved with the Dutchman Karel, the Spaniard Paco and the possibility of owning our own *cortijo*.

El Cortijuelo

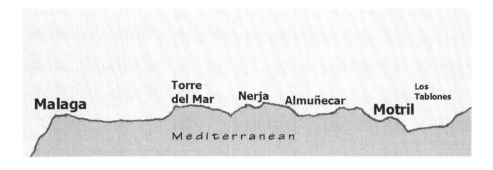

CHAPTER FOUR
Paco's Bar

The drive to Los Tablones on our second visit - November 1988 - was completely straightforward, making us wonder why it had been so difficult the first time.

As previously mentioned, this is when we met the Dutch couple, Karel and Eva, who were staying in Roger's house. They had been travelling for several months around the south of Spain looking for somewhere to set down roots and this was their chosen area. Their aim was to find a cottage with some land where they could grow fruit and vegetables and be self-sufficient. Because of the surrounding mountains, Karel said that Los Tablones had a unique micro-climate that was perfect for cultivation all year round.

During the conversation, we mentioned that we had been fantasizing about owning one of the abandoned cottages dotted about the hills and turning it into a holiday home. A few days later, he mentioned the little ruin that was for sale. And that is how we came to be on the road to Motril, following Karel in his Jeep, to talk to the owner, Paco, about a possible purchase.

Apparently, the road we normally used to Motril was the long way round. Those in the know used a shorter route that involved leaving the tarmac road and bumping down a short incline into a *rio seco* (dry riverbed). A quarter of a mile or so further on, one was able to climb out again and join the main road into Motril. All the locals went this way except in the rainy season when torrents of water poured down from the mountains and the *rio* became far from *seco*. It was a quite a rough ride in our small hire car requiring concentration to avoid hitting large stones and pieces of rock along the way, but it was certainly quicker. Soon we were in Motril and parking outside Paco's Bar, a typical restaurant/bar on the corner of a busy street.

The interior was long and thin with the bar running down the left hand side, opening into a wider space at the end where there was an eating area. Paco and two assistants were busy behind the bar serving a crowd of people. He indicated that we should wait at one of the tables in the restaurant. It was empty at this time of night, being far too early for most Spaniards to eat.

The majority of Spanish country folk born prior to the 1960s are short and square, unlike subsequent generations who, benefiting from an improving economy with better healthcare and diet, are noticeably taller and slimmer. Paco, being in his forties, was hardly more than five feet tall. He had a round, smiley, weather-beaten face and wore black round-framed glasses. The strong lenses magnified his eyes, which was slightly disturbing when he stared at you.

Soon, the rush at the bar died down and he joined us at the table bringing bread and *jamon serrano* (dry cured ham) thinly sliced from a leg fixed to a rack sitting on the counter. Served on square wooden platters, the ham was quite chewy, but delicious with the warm fresh crusty bread. He also organized drinks for us before settling down to business.

Karel explained that we were definitely interested in the *cortijo* he was selling, but it all depended upon the price.

Paco shrugged and spread his hands in a "but of course" gesture before launching into a lot of words ending in *miliones* and *pesetas*. Seeing the blank looks on our faces, he produced a felt-tip pen and wrote on the paper tablecloth: 1,500,000 pesetas. That was a shock. So many naughts! We were aware of the exchange rate, but without a calculator, had difficulty grappling with the figures. It appeared to be just over £7,000. Or was it £70,000? Surely a cottage with all that land could not be as little as £7,000. In the UK that was the price of a decent second hand car. On the other hand, £70,000 seemed far too much. Karel set our minds at rest. It was definitely the lower figure. This was too good to be true. Even with our limited resources, it was affordable. I knew I could come up with £5,000 and Alison said she could lay her hands on the rest.

Paco, noticing the relief on our faces, confided something to Karel before writing another figure on the tablecloth. The amount he wrote was 150,000 pesetas. Karel nodded and explained that, as was normal in Spain, Paco required 10% in cash in order to secure the property.

This we had not foreseen. There was no way we could come up with that amount before leaving the following afternoon. We did not have a Spanish bank account and our holiday money was down to just a few pounds. Our predicament was relayed to Paco whose reply, in translation, was that other people had shown interest in the property and not being able to come up with the deposit was a major obstacle.

To further complicate matters, Alison came up with another stumbling block. Before our departure, there would be no time to visit a lawyer and do whatever was necessary to make the whole thing legal.

Karel explained that it was not necessary to see a lawyer at this stage. The sale was agreed once the owner had signed a receipt for the deposit. Then, when the full purchase price was paid, a simple purchase agreement was signed and witnessed by both parties. It was at this point that a lawyer was called upon to register the transaction. This involved a great deal of bureaucracy. Documents had to be drawn up and sent to Madrid for ratification and this always took many weeks. All this, however, was a formality that could be sorted out at a later date. The important part, the actual purchase agreement, was not a problem as he, Karel, could handle this for us.

Nevertheless, this did not solve the immediate problem of cash. All seemed hopeless. Shoulders were shrugged, apologetic glances exchanged, beer was drunk – or coffee in Alison's case as she dislikes alcohol. Then Karel perked up. He had an idea. He might be able to help.

"How would it be if I lend you the deposit money and then you reimburse me as soon as you get home? I can give you my bank details."

"No, we couldn't possibly do that. I mean, you hardly know us."

"Look, I am friend of Roger and you are friends of Roger. Friends can be trusted."

"That is very kind and we would be grateful, but how do we pay the rest of the money? I am sure that Paco will not want to wait until we come to Spain again. It could be up to a year."

"Can you not get here sooner?"

"It's unlikely."

"Oh my. That is a big problem. In Spanish law the full amount must be paid within six weeks or the agreement is off. You lose the deposit. Sorry, there is no way round this."

Karel seemed as disappointed as we were. On the other hand, perhaps it was just as well. To tell the truth, it was almost a relief. The whole thing had become too fraught with difficulties and unknown complications. It had been a madcap idea anyway and when back in England and living in the real world, we would probably look upon it as a lucky escape.

Karel explained the situation to Paco who nodded sadly, pursing his lips. Once again, shoulders were shrugged. Then Karel had another idea:

"There is one way I could help, if you agree. I could get the purchase agreement drawn up by a lawyer - I know a good one - then, as soon as I have the agreement we speak on the telephone. If you send the money to my bank, I will meet the lawyer with Paco, he signs the agreement and I pass on the money. The deal is done. It is all legal.

"That is a very kind of you, but we cannot put you to all that trouble."

"I did not really want to get involved with the money, but if it helps you and you wish to go ahead, this is possible."

"No, it is out of the question, really."

"Look, Eva and I are determined to fine a place to live around this area, so I will be here anyway and it is not so much trouble. If you are really sure you want to buy the *cortijo*, it is my pleasure. If not, that is not a problem. We forget it. Paco will understand. Take a while to think about it. It is a big step."

We were getting in too deep. It was far too complicated and definitely not a good idea. We thought about it - for about ten seconds. Then, with smiles all round, everyone was shaking hands and the deal was done. More drinks were summoned and we all toasted each other, then toasted *Inglaterra*, then toasted *España*, then toasted several other things we knew not the what of, but it did not matter. Thanks to our Dutch friend, we were about to become the owners of a little piece of paradise in Andalucia.

CHAPTER FIVE
La Caracola

During the drive back to Los Tablones, after saying goodbye to Karel and Paco, the magnitude of what we had agreed began to hit us. On the one hand it was totally irresponsible; on the other hand, the more we discussed ideas for our little ruin, the more exciting the project appeared.

We had decided to return the way we had been shown via the *rio seco*, but were so distracted making plans, that we thought we might have missed the narrow track that led to the riverbed. It was daylight when we had followed Karel and neither of us had paid much attention. Now it was dark and things looked different. We stopped at several likely tracks but could not see where they led; possibly to someone's house. A decision had to be made, so we took a likely turning and soon came to a steep stony slope and, hallelujah, the car slithered into the riverbed. After negotiating the boulders and ruts in the ground for what seemed far too long, I mentioned my concern. Perhaps it just seemed longer because we were on our own and in the dark. That must be it. Minutes passed as we continued bumping along the rough terrain. Then Alison had a worrying thought:

"Do you think…?"

"Do I think what?"

"Do you think we could be driving up the wrong riverbed?"

There was a moment's pause. Then we both exploded with laughter, the tears running down our cheeks. A wonderful relief of tension. As if the ludicrous events of the evening were not sufficient, what on earth were these two English idiots doing, in the dead of night, driving a little hire car along a riverbed – in Spain?

Recovering our composure, we agreed to continue for a while and within a minute or two the steep little track that took us out of the riverbed came into view. Soon we were on the familiar road to Los Tablones to spend our last night in *El Cortijuelo*.

The following morning, before heading to Malaga airport, we went for a last look at "our property". According to Paco, the *cortijo* actually had a name - *La*

29

Caracola. In Spanish a *caracol* is a snail and *La Caracola* means "The Snail Lady". Apparently, the last person to live in the house, some ten or fifteen years previously, was an elderly lady who collected edible snails and sold them in Almuñécar's municipal market. This knowledge somehow made our little cottage even more special. We could never have invented such a romantic name as *La Caracola* and now we were going to bring The Snail Lady's dwelling back to life.

By six o'clock in the evening we had driven to the airport, dumped the hire car, and were flying across Spain on the way to Gatwick, able to relax at last. It had been an eventful two days and, not for the first time, the discussion revolved around whether or not we had talked ourselves into a situation we would come to regret. Could the whole episode have been a scam? How many times had we heard tales of Brits on holiday, carried away with the sunshine and the lifestyle, investing in some property which they later discovered they did not own, or was about to be bulldozed to make way for a road?

Happily, we were reassured in the knowledge that Roger trusted Karel and Eva to live in his house and if they were up to anything underhand, it was bound to be revealed sooner or later. Also, Paco was Roger's neighbour and another friend.

By the time the plane landed at Gatwick airport, we had reconciled ourselves to the fact that the die was cast and we just had to cross our fingers and stop worrying. After all, if the whole thing fell apart, the very worst outcome would be the loss of the £700 deposit. That would be incredibly annoying but not the end of the world. Admittedly, the whole venture was crazy, but sometimes being a little crazy is what makes life interesting.

At the airport, we were met by Alison's father who drove us back to the family home where we had left our car. Although bursting to reveal the exciting news, we waited until we were sitting round the dinner table with both Alison's parents. Her father, an academic, always treated me with courtesy and good humour but I never felt completely at ease in his presence. He was a patriarchal figure of the old school and I always had to restrain myself from addressing him as Sir. The life he led was very ordered and abstemious except for two uncharacteristic indulgences; one was a bright red Mazda sports car and the other was a full size snooker table which, because of its weight, occupied one of the two main rooms on the ground floor. The other room, the most pleasant in the house with French windows leading on to the garden, he had bagged for his study. This meant that the living and dining rooms were relegated to the first floor, not terribly convenient for the kitchen below.

Alison's mother was a warm smiley person with a twinkle in her eye and a smoker's throaty laugh. Always unruffled, she ran the house and managed her husband calmly and methodically while fighting a constant battle with the household finances. Her weekly allowance had been meticulously calculated by the professor and was deemed to be sufficient for all essentials. This meant that corners had to be cut if she needed to buy anything for herself - like clothes. This partnership of dependable breadwinner and efficient housewife was typical of middle class marriages of the 1940s and 50s. To us, in the 1980s, it seemed an unacceptable and outmoded way of life, but they appeared content with the arrangement.

Knowing all this, we anticipated expressions of surprise and even concern when revealing our commitment to purchase a ruin and half a hillside in Spain, but we did not expect the news to be greeted with such appalled expressions followed by a stunned silence.

Upon reflection, instead of blurting it out, we should have led up to the revelation more gently by describing the spectacular countryside around Los Tablones and how our friends had bought ruins out there and turned them into spectacular houses, and how cheap everything was, and what a good investment they had made. Our error was to state the bare facts without filling in any of the background. Now, having assimilated this bombshell, crossing their minds must have been their daughter's association with this older divorcee who had responsibilities and not much money. How were they to know if this was a serious relationship? We had only discovered it ourselves a few days earlier.

Alison tried to lighten the atmosphere by relating how the negotiations had taken place in a bar with the price written on a paper table cloth, and how we had not been sure whether the millions of pesetas converted to £7,000 or £70,000 and how we were so relieved when it was the lower figure.

The anecdote did not go down well. If anything, it increased their concern. Frittering away such a sum was unthinkable. Alison's mother just shook her head and looked worried while her father, breaking the grim silence, began asking questions about legally binding contracts, witnesses, Spanish laws regarding foreigners owning property, tax implications, and money. Also, how were we actually going to renovate the property with little time available to spend in the country and no knowledge of the language? None of which we were able to answer convincingly – or at all.

It was a sticky hour or so before we were able to excuse ourselves and take our leave. Duly chastened, we headed back to the houseboat.

The next day we arranged for our bank to send the £700 deposit to our Dutch friend in Spain. Later the same day, I telephoned Tony and Monique in Paris with the news and although they were mightily surprised, their positive reaction helped to restore our confidence. We were told that *El Cortijuelo* would always be available to us.

CHAPTER SIX
Change of Life-Style

Not long after agreeing to buy the ruin, there were some great upheavals in my working life. I had been asked to replace the managing director of the group of companies I had been with for more than twenty years. My task was to slim down and sell off various activities in order to repay the crippling bank loans. In some cases this involved the unpleasant task of making friends and colleagues redundant. Somehow, we managed to survive but with the group reduced to just one company, this being the very successful consultancy operation that was involved in the design of theatres and arts centres around the world. One of the most prestigious projects had been the National Theatre on the South Bank for which I had specified all the sound and communications systems. With a thriving office in New York as well as London, Theatre Projects Consultants Limited was the world's most successful company in its field, with contracts in more than sixty countries.

Following several months of sitting in an office worrying about finance and administration, I was desperate to get back to doing something more creative. I could have continued as a consultant designing sound systems, but sitting at a desk writing specifications, with long hours at a drawing board and tedious meetings with clients and architects, was not the sort of life envisaged when I had chosen a theatrical career. It was time for a change.

Alison also wished to change her life-style. Since we had first met at the Polka Children's Theatre, she had performed in several other productions including playing Ophelia in "Rosencrantz and Guildenstern Are Dead" in the West End. However, she became disenchanted with the prospect of spending her life constantly auditioning for new parts. The answer was to write and perform her own plays. In 1988, she premiered her first one-woman show, "Bella - The Story of Mrs Beeton". This proved a great success and launched a new career creating plays based on the lives of interesting women and touring them to small theatres and village halls around the country.

With a colleague from Theatre Projects as financial director, David Pelham, we set up a company called Adventure Projects to design and manage historically themed visitor centres. These would be full of lighting, sound, video, and all kinds of theatrical effects. All these technical installations were brilliantly handled by another friend from the old company. Within a few years, we had designed permanent attractions for a number of clients and were managing several operations of our own including an aquarium and a permanent exhibition in Hastings, "A Smugglers Adventure", set in an acre and a half of caves. Alison assisted with the research for all these projects, enjoying the process so much that she set up a second career as a writer and researcher. Commissions for her talents included major events such as the Royal Tournament and the VE Day celebrations in Hyde Park, plus a number of castles and other historical sites.

Most importantly, finding the Spanish ruin had cemented our relationship and we were now in the process of setting up home together. My houseboat was too cramped for two people who were trying to run separate businesses, so as we no longer needed to be based in London, we decided to move to the country. By chance, a friend wished to purchase the houseboat and was keen to move in as soon as possible. As a temporary measure, until we could find a suitable house to buy, we arranged to rent a property near the small town of Brackley in Buckinghamshire. I began to pack.

Meanwhile, having allowed a week for the £700 to reach Karel's bank account, it was time to ask if he it had been successfully transferred.

With some trepidation, Alison beside me for support, I telephoned the Flamingo Hotel in Almuñécar at 7.00 p.m. as arranged. I was to say: "*Ola. Por favor, hablo con Karel Holandes?*" (Hello, please I speak with Dutch Karel?) and trust that he was there and hope that the person answering did not have any wish to discuss the matter. As a precaution, we consulted the Spanish dictionary and had in readiness: "*Lo siento, no hablo español. Adios.*" (Sorry, I do not speak Spanish. Goodbye) after which I would quickly replace the receiver.

The telephone was answered by a female voice shouting against a hubbub of background chatter:

"*diga me.*" (speak to me).

This was obviously the bar. I said my line and when she shouted something in reply, all I could do was remain silent and wait to see what would happen. Following a long pause listening to the noise in the bar, it was a relief to recognise a warm comforting voice:

"Hello David. This is Karel."

"Oh, good. Hello. I am just ringing to make sure the money arrived."

"Yes, I have it."

"Great."

"And now, David, I am seeing the lawyer to make an agreement. Paco will sign this and then I will give him the money. When this is done, you must then send the rest of the money so that the *cortijo* can be transferred into your name."

"Thank you. We are very grateful."

"No problem. I will send you a fax when Paco has signed the agreement. Eva and I look forward to seeing you when you next come to Spain."

The fax arrived ten days later, by which time we were busy moving into the rented property in Bracknell.

CHAPTER SEVEN
Problems With The Bank

So it was that Alison and I found ourselves one morning visiting a bank in Brackley High Street to transfer roughly £6,300 into Karel's account. Not such a problem you would think, as it was our money in our account and this was a branch of the bank we always used in London. But no, it was too large a sum to send to a foreign country without authorisation from London. OK, we said, get them on the telephone.

"We cannot do that. You have to speak to them."

"All right, get them on the telephone and we will speak to them."

"I am sorry, but customers are not permitted to use the bank telephone."

"This is ridiculous. It is <u>our</u> money, you are holding in your bank, and we wish to transfer it <u>now</u>. So what are you going to do about it?"

"There is a phone box just across the street."

Fuming, we marched out into the pouring rain to look for the phone box. Trying to make the phone call and slot in 10p coins every few minutes whilst juggling the bank file and details of the Spanish bank was not easy. Not helped by the fact that the phone box was not large enough for the two of us. The door could not be closed, so not only were we battling with the traffic noise from the High Street, but we were getting wet.

The person in the London bank who listened patiently to our request, pointed out that authorisation was not necessary as the local branch was perfectly able to make the transfer. Eventually, we persuaded him to send a fax to the local branch, containing all the necessary details and permissions.

Twenty minutes later, we were informed by the official in the local bank that the fax had arrived and the money was now winging its way to Spain. Job done. Hardly a problem at all.

A few days passed, giving sufficient time for the money to arrive, before I telephoned the Flamingo Hotel in Almuñécar at 7.00 p.m. once again. Karel said that I could always contact him there at that time, but I was a little apprehensive as I dialed and the female voice shouted:

"*diga me.*"

Olu. Por favor, hablo con Karel Holandes?

This time she said nothing. Then, after a short pause:

"Hello David. This is Karel."

"Hello Karel. Have you received the money?"

"No. I went to my bank yesterday and today. There is nothing and they say that there is no transfer in the pipeline."

"It should have been with you a day or two ago. I will check with my bank and let you know what is happening tomorrow."

Alison, being much tougher than I with banks and similar inefficient organisations, offered to contact our London bank and demanded to know why there had been this delay. Refusing to accept the assurance by two different people that she was not to worry, that the money had been sent and was certain to arrive shortly, she insisted on talking to someone who could provide facts and not talk platitudes. Eventually, she was passed to the Foreign Exchange department and the man answering, when pushed, agreed to look into the matter and report back.

When he called later that day, his answer was less than helpful. As far as they were concerned, the money had been transferred, it was in Spain, and the bank was no longer responsible. Alison hit the roof. This was completely unacceptable. Nothing had been received by the Spanish bank and he was saying that his bank no longer had it! So where was it? If the money had been lost, he better get on to Spain right now and find out what had happened. She would not let the man go until he reluctantly agreed to "see what he could do". That evening I contacted Karel at the hotel to inform him about the delay with assurances that it would soon be resolved.

During the following two days, there were more heated phone conversations with the bank who finally admitted that the funds, which had now been missing for several days, seemed to have gone astray. Surprisingly, when Alison enquired if they had actually spoken to the Spanish bank, she was told that it was not possible because nobody in the office spoke Spanish. This was a statement from the Foreign Exchange department of one of the country's largest banks, a fact pointed out by Alison with a great deal of pith. Totally shamed by her tirade - one hoped - some way of communicating with Spain was found because the final phone call, later that day, informed us that the funds had now arrived at the Spanish bank. No explanation or even an apology was forthcoming.

I once again braved the telephone and the *Hablo con Karel Holandes* routine. The same lady answered and Karel soon came to the phone. The money had finally arrived at the bank, but there was some difficulty about transferring it into his account. Perhaps if I phoned back in two days time, it would have been sorted. However, there was good news.

"My lawyer has given me a copy of the agreement in your name. I will send it to you when we receive the money. The deeds can be collected from the lawyer when you next come to Spain."

Everything seemed to be going according to plan, but when I made the next telephone call to the Flamingo Hotel, Karel was still having problems accessing the money.

Because it was a relatively large amount from a foreign source, they were suspicious that something dodgy was going on, perhaps money laundering. They simply refused to give him access. The only way round this latest obstacle would be for us to give him a letter of Power of Attorney. Did we know of a lawyer in England who dealt with Spanish matters? I said that I would look into it immediately.

A Spanish firm of lawyers was located in London who said they could set up a Power of Attorney, but this meant visiting their office. However, there was no time to arrange anything before we received a surprise phone call from Roger. There being no telephones in Los Tablones, he was calling from a restaurant he often frequented on the road to Motril.

He had just returned from Paris where our mutual friends Tony and Monique had told him of our involvement with Karel in the purchase of the *cortijo*. He asked if this was true? I confirmed that it was indeed the case and his friend Karel was being most helpful. Roger's response was something we really did not wish to hear.

"Oh my God! I'm sorry to tell you this, but you are being taken for a complete ride. Karel and Eva are not friends of mine. I hardly know them. They were paying guests in one of my houses and I let them stay on while we were away, rather than have the place empty. This is a disaster. Tell me exactly what you have done."

I related the whole story and when I reached the bit about giving Karel Power of Attorney, he was appalled.

"You realise that a Power of Attorney would have given him access to all your money? He could have made off with the lot! Look, leave it to me for a couple of days and I will call you back. Meanwhile, <u>do nothing</u>."

I relayed the gist of the conversation to Alison. The look on her face said everything. It took us both a few moments for the enormity of the situation to sink in and realise how Roger, in the nick of time, had saved us from a total disaster. And then did we feel fools?

As good as his word, Roger was able to rescue us from most of the mess. The first thing he did was to visit the bank and tell them not to release the money to Karel under any circumstances. This included not only the main sum but also the deposit that was still in his account. We wondered how on earth he had managed to achieve this with somebody else's bank account. Perhaps he was friendly with the bank manager or did he know one of the staff? As he explained later:

"*Know* the boys in the bank? I dance with them."

Before throwing the Dutch couple off his property, Roger had a blazing row, accusing them of cheating and attempting to steal money from one of his friends while, at the same time, abusing his hospitality. Karel's defence was that it was a business deal and everyone was happy with the arrangement. Nobody was getting hurt. The final straw was when Karel tried to dismiss the whole thing by saying:

"Everybody knows the English are gullible. That is not my fault."

Roger was incensed and, suspecting that they had been working similar scams along the coast, reported the incident to the Spanish police, suggesting that their passports be marked as 'undesirables'. We understand that the couple left Spain shortly afterwards with little chance of returning.

That was all very satisfactory, but Roger had more bombshells to release: firstly, *La Caracola* did not actually belong to his friend Paco. Roger knew this because he was acquainted with the rightful owner. Secondly, Karel had almost doubled the asking price. Obviously Paco was in it up to his neck. After all, he had written the price on the tablecloth in the bar, but he was insisting that he had been given the right to sell the property.

It was decision time. Did we still want to proceed with the project at all, despite the fact that Paco would still be involved? If so, did we want Roger to tackle him about the asking price? The difficulty for Roger was not wishing to accuse Paco of fraud, thereby falling out with a close neighbour.

We had thought, and still thought, that £7,000 for the *cortijo* with all that land was a bargain. So, to save Roger any embarrassment there was only one practical answer. We decided to pretend that the events of the past weeks had never happened and proceed with the purchase at the original price.

CHAPTER EIGHT
Back At Paco's Bar

When the sorry story was relayed to friends Tony and Monique, they suggested that we join them at *El Cortijuelo* on their next trip; an invitation we were only too happy to accept. So, a couple of months later found us once again in Los Tablones and thanking Roger in person for his spectacular efforts on our behalf.

A meeting that was set up to discuss the purchase of *La Caracola* turned out to be a bizarre replay of the previous event in Paco's Bar; only this time, instead of the Dutchman seated next to Paco, there was the reassuring presence of Roger.

Paco, ignoring the fact that Roger had replaced Karel at the meeting, showed no sign of shame or remorse. On the contrary, he seemed incredibly pleased with himself. And why not? Now that Karel was out of the picture, he would presumably be doubling his profit. Of course, none of this was referred to then or, indeed, later. What happened in Paco's Bar stayed in Paco's Bar.

Roger began by explaining how Paco was kindly acting as a go-between us and the owner and had ascertained that there was no problem with the sale. So now we needed to visit a lawyer to handle the money, draw up a proper contract and arrange transfer of the title deeds. Paco, regarding us through his lenses with those big eyes, nodded his agreement and indicated his eagerness to assist. Through gritted teeth, we were forced to declare our gratitude. Then, in a weird reenactment of a similar scene, everyone raised their glasses to the new owners of *La Caracola*.

Accepting our thanks with a dismissive gesture, Paco turned to have a short conversation with Roger. It transpired that he was concerned about vandals, and to secure the place until we could take possession, as a neighbourly gesture he was offering to board up the windows and doors and repair some crumbling brickwork. We thanked him again.

Not surprisingly, the little bit of work so generously offered to secure the house never happened, but all of the original floor tiles that still remained when we first saw the cottage mysteriously disappeared. Fortunately, Roger had already rescued the chest and bedhead that belonged to the house and were very much part of its history.

An appointment was made with the *abogado* (lawyer) used by Tony and Monique when they purchased *El Cortijuelo*. Having a good grasp of Spanish, Monique agreed to come along and translate. The office in the centre of Motril was in an imposing modern block; cool interior with white walls, white marble floors and staircases with white balustrades.

Abogado Juan Alvarez was compact, medium height, sporting a dark blue tailored suit with just enough white cuff showing to reveal chunky gold cufflinks and an expensive gold watch. Black hair neatly trimmed, manicured fingernails, and a welcoming smile revealed a set of perfect white teeth. In short, the right sort of image to instill confidence in one's lawyer.

Monique explained the situation and we set before him names and addresses and details of the transaction. Having taken this in, he sat back and regarded us for some while with eyebrows raised. His whole demeanour indicated that agreements made with strangers in bars, in his experience would be fraught with all kinds of unforeseen problems. But then his face broke into a broad smile and with a dismissive wave of the hand, we understood that, for an *abogado* of his caliber, sorting this out was all in a day's work.

We were told to meet him the following morning at the office of the *notario* (notary) to be found on the ground floor of this building. The sale agreement, which he would have prepared for us, had to be signed in front of a *notario*. Juan Alvarez would arrange for the seller to sign on another occasion.

It was impressed upon us that whenever the *notario* asked a question we were to say *"si"*. This was vital, because if he twigged that we did not understand what we were signing, the session would be cancelled. The whole procedure would obviously be carried out in Spanish and, unfortunately, Monique would not be free to accompany us.

At the appointed hour, we waited nervously in the ante room to the *notario's* office until we were ushered into the presence of a middle aged man with horn-rimmed spectacles seated behind a large leather-topped desk. With a curt gesture, the *notario* indicated that we should be seated. Juan Alvarez remained standing as he reverentially handed over our case file. All was silent except for the rustling of papers as the files were studied. The *notario* asked a few questions to which Alvarez replied. All communication was carried out in hushed tones. It felt like being up before the Head for some misdemeanor with our Form Master doing his best to explain our behaviour.

Then the *notario* looked directly at us and said:

"Pasaportes."

"Si."

We were ready for this one and quickly produced our passports. These were checked against the names on the sale agreement before the *notario* began to read it out aloud, occasionally pausing to enquire something of us, to which we dutifully replied:

"Si."

Finally, the *notario* swiveled the document round towards us saying:

"Firmar, por favor."

"Si."

There was just a moment of potential embarrassment before Juan Alvarez stepped forward with his pen and indicated that we were being told to append our signatures. This being done, the *notario* stood up and, smiling for the first time, proffered his hand to Alison and then to me while saying something that sounded encouraging. I replied with my most emphatic *"Si"* and Alison threw in a *"Muchas Gracias"* for good measure – which was not in the script, but seemed to go down well.

As soon as we had walked out of the office and the door was safely closed, the atmosphere lightened. Smiles all round. *La Caracola* was ours at last. All that remained was for the sale agreement to be sent to Granada for official ratification, a formality that would be processed automatically, and a new *escritura de propiedad* (Title Deed) would be issued. We would then officially own the property. The only possible stumbling block, as had previously been explained, was in the unlikely event that some distant relation of the owner turned up with a claim to the property.

All that remained was to hand over a cheque to our friendly *abogado*, which was no problem as we now had a Spanish bank account into which the money originally sent out to Karel had been transferred. So, to this end, we returned to his office on the third floor.

In our copy of the agreement, we discovered that the *"La Caracola"* was only part of the official name of the property. The full title ran as follows: *La Caracola, el pecho de Torrelejo, Los Tablones.* Roger translated this as: The snail lady, the breast of the far away tower, The Planks. Since there was no far away tower to be seen and no one knew why Los Tablones was called The Planks (literal translation), this was all splendidly arcane.

The legal side being done and dusted, we returned to tell Roger the good news and thank him once again. Suitably relieved, he then proceeded to make our day complete with another piece of good news. Most of the restoration work on their own houses had been finished and Robert was suggesting that he should undertake the building work on our *cortijo*. We were overwhelmed and pathetically grateful.

During the next few days Robert prepared a quotation that included building a *deposito* (big water tank) and, once there was water on site, cleaning, cementing and painting all the interior walls, laying a new floor with traditional rustic tiles, adding new doors and windows, building a kitchen and bathroom and generally making the place habitable. The price he quoted for all this work was unbelievable. It amounted to less than £2,000.

At a final meeting on site to discuss details, Robert was accompanied by Miguel, a builder who was to assist him with the project. A large muscular mountain of a man with a granite face sprouting thick black stubble, piercing brown eyes and set lips that never seemed to smile. Our introduction was favoured with a brief nod. The hand I tentatively proffered was, to my relief, ignored as I was imagining crushed bones.

One wondered how this unlikely duo would spend their days working together. The trim figure of Robert with his interest in art and design and this dour giant of a man made a very odd couple. On the other hand, one could appreciate the practical advantages on a building site of such a combination of brain and brawn.

Everything was extremely satisfactory. The following day, we were able to depart for the UK in the knowledge that *La Caracola* was officially ours and, before long, would be undergoing a much-needed facelift. The horrors of the past weeks could be put behind us.

Perhaps, in retrospect, one should have kept in mind that old adage concerning the counting of chickens.

CHAPTER NINE
Miguel

It was some months before there was an opportunity to return to Los Tablones. I had become busy designing exhibitions and visitor centres while Alison was involved in the historical and picture research for these projects as well as for other clients. The bookings for her one-woman play about Mrs Beeton had increased and she was now investigating suitable characters for a second show.

While we were renting the house in Brackley and looking for a suitable property to buy, it came to our attention that there was an old houseboat for sale on Taggs Island where my previous houseboat had been moored. It had a small garden and the mooring was big enough to replace the old boat with a larger new one. I was missing life on the river and properties on Taggs Island did not come on the market very often. We nipped back to London and, because we had cash available from the sale of my old houseboat, were able to do a deal. Then came the fun of specifying the new boat and designing the interior to our particular requirements.

Because of all this activity, it was not until March of 1990, eighteen months after Karel had first shown us *La Caracola*, that we both managed to free up a few days for a short visit to Spain.

Our excitement at the thought of seeing what progress had been made on our little house was somewhat dampened when we drew up at Roger's house and found him in a state of deep depression. Although it was a warm sunny day – shirtsleeve weather – he was indoors slumped in a chair with a scarf around his neck looking extremely unwell. No cheery welcome. In fact, he hardly acknowledged our presence. Just a dreary "Oh hello" as though we were the last people he wanted to see. By exchange of letter, we had been invited to stay in one of his houses, but it now felt as though we were unwelcome intruders. I asked him if he was sick and if we could do anything to help. Reluctantly rousing himself and slowly managing to sit upright, he apologized and explained that he was in a low state. "Life is awful", he groaned.

"Why? What's the matter? Can we help?"

"He's gone."

"Who's gone?"

"Robert."

"Gone where?"

"I don't know. They just disappeared."

"They?"

"Robert and Miguel."

"What do you mean?"

"They have run off together. Robert and Miguel."

"Robert and Miguel?"

"Abandoned his wife and six children and gone off with Robert."

"But… Miguel? That big burly builder?"

"They've gone. Robert has gone. After all I have done for him. How could he do this to me?"

He sank back into his chair, pulling the scarf tightly around his neck for comfort. We commiserated and tried to offer cheer but the poor man was inconsolable. As he showed no signs of escorting us to our accommodation, we suggested sorting ourselves out. No comment was forthcoming so, assuming we were to be in the same house as before, we headed off. Nothing was prepared, but we knew where the bed linen was kept and how to turn on the bottled gas, so were soon settled in.

Later, when we caught up with Roger and he felt able to speak, he explained that, before walking out, Robert and "that man" had managed to build our *deposito*. This meant that we could at least have water delivered to the site for whoever was going to continue the building work. Roger had been in charge of ordering the materials and had paid for quite a lot of sand, cement and iron for reinforcing. Reimbursing him was not a problem. The question was: who was going to continue the renovation?

Roger, still stunned by Robert's betrayal, was in no state to think about builders. He was consumed with the knowledge that the idyllic world they had created together was now in tatters. How could he maintain and rent out the holiday homes and look after all the land on his own? And, anyhow, what was the point?

Leaving Roger deep in the Slough of Despond, Alison and I trudged up to the abandoned *Caracola* where we discovered that the *deposito* built by Robert and Miguel was really excellent – much larger than we had imagined and with a concrete hutch protruding from the far end to house the pump. They had also cleared the debris inside the house and cleaned off the flaking paintwork from the walls. Somewhat cheered by this, we decided to continue with the clean-up operation during the remainder of our stay. We only had two more clear days in Spain, so there was not enough time to find a builder, even if we knew where to look.

The first item to be tackled was the main feature in the living room - the *chiminea*. When we started tapping nervously at the mantelpiece, great chunks of paint, up to 6cm thick, fell off. Coats of whitewash must have been applied one on top of the other year after year.

Water tank *(Deposito)* on the left

At first we feared we were destroying the whole structure, but gradually all the shelves and surfaces that had been lumpy and uneven with rounded edges were revealed as being beautifully crafted, slim, and angular. An enormous quantity of paint was removed in a totally satisfying way. This, we thought, is what an archaeologist must feel when chipping away to uncover some ancient Roman relic.

Both days saw small improvements, not least was revealing the tiled surface above the 'bottle rack' holes to the left of the fireplace. As Karel had forecast, above one of the cavities where hot embers would have been placed, there was a solid tile acting as a hot-plate. Above the other opening was indeed a tile with a hole in it to accommodate a round-bottomed cooking pot.

All too soon, the visit came to an end. Although some progress had been made to the little *cortijo*, there were major works ahead that we had neither the time nor the skills to attempt.

On the flight home, we formulated a plan. At that time, 1990, it was difficult to find any English speakers in the Motril area, but the seaside town of Nerja (pronounced 'Nairca'), a good forty minutes nearer Malaga airport, was a popular tourist resort with a sizeable community of ex-pats. Consequently, as the English seem incapable of learning a second language, many hotels, shops and businesses had found it necessary to become bi-lingual. Surely, with the number of new houses springing up around the town, there must be builders who spoke English.

CHAPTER TEN
The Search For An English Builder

During the next few months, I was to be totally involved in the design and installation of our new audio-visual attraction at Hastings Castle, plus preparing a major exhibition for the city of Rotterdam. However, Alison had a few days available and volunteered to fly out. For moral support, she persuaded her mother that it would be a jolly adventure and, once again, booked one of Roger's houses. Major technical advance: Roger now had a satellite telephone. It was about the size and weight of a brick with an enormously long aerial but communication became much easier.

Towards the end of May, Alison arrived in Malaga with her mother. Having never driven on the right hand side of the road before, the journey from the airport was tense with her mother making nervous comments as traffic approached or passed on the wrong side. It did not help that the temperature was in the mid 80s (27° plus) and the hire car had no air conditioning.

The heat continued to be a problem throughout their week in Los Tablones. They had trouble sleeping at nights, often being disturbed by the high whine of a mosquito. On one occasion, when switching on the light to locate the annoying insect, Alison's mother screamed out when she saw a gecko scuttling across the ceiling. We had become used to these weird little lizards and Alison explained that they were harmless; information that did nothing to calm a person whose home was a no-go area for any form of life whatsoever that was not human. When she complained to Roger that she had no wish to be woken in the night by a fat lizard falling on her face, he merely sighed and explained that geckos never lost their grip - well not often. Alison's mother was unimpressed.

"Of course, there are creatures around here that should be avoided. For example, there is a big centipede – bright red - if you come across one of those, just get out of the way quick. They move like lightening and have really nasty stings - many times worse than a scorpion. Fortunately, like snakes, they only come into a house by mistake – perhaps looking for somewhere cool. In fact, I had a strange experience last summer when I was about to get out of bed one morning. Half asleep, I was feeling on the floor for my slippers when I touched something that moved. I sat up sharply, now wide awake, and discovered that I had just put my hand on a scorpion. Would you believe it? I think it was as surprised as I was, which is probably why it did not sting me. I managed to kill it and I still have it in a jam jar, if you would like to see it."

Alison's mother certainly did not wish to see it. Born and bred in London, she had never seen the point of living in the country and this short stay in a Spanish country cottage did nothing to change her view. In her firm opinion, anywhere without a proper tarmac road, decent pavements and streetlights should be avoided.

Her reaction, therefore, on first viewing *La Caracola* was not entirely unexpected. Incomprehension would probably sum it up. She could not believe they had come all the way to Spain for this broken down hovel, miles from civilization, set in an unpleasant rocky landscape. Why on earth would anyone in their right mind wish to own a pokey little ruin with no proper floors and crumbling walls made of mud? And being on the edge of a cliff it was just plain dangerous.

Alison enquired how on earth it could be dangerous. The answer was obvious. With no streetlights it would be pitch black at night, so if you came out of the house and turned the wrong way by mistake, well...!

Alison tried to explain our exciting plans for renovating the house, but to no avail. Amicably agreeing to differ, they decided to turn their attention to the job in hand.

An exhausting morning was spent walking the streets of Nerja searching in vain for a builder who spoke English. Even a Builders Merchant, which you would think an obvious place to ask, was not able to come up with anything. The man they accosted, who was hauling bags of cement into a white van, understood what they were looking for but he just shook his head and shrugged his shoulders. The woman in the Tourist Information Centre did speak English but was equally unhelpful - and seemed quite pleased about it.

The temperature in the middle of the day was uncomfortably hot and as businesses and shops, other than restaurants and cafes, close from 2.00 p.m. until 5.00 p.m. they returned to the house for a siesta before setting off again on another fruitless search. Later that evening, exhausted, they gave up and retired to a restaurant. Alison found a cockroach in her tortilla, but did not think it necessary to trouble her mother with the news.

The schedule for the following day in Nerja included an hour or two relaxing on the beach during siesta time. They had noticed an attractive little bay with umbrellas for shade and delicious ice creams on hand to keep one cool. The sea was warm enough for a swim and this very pleasant interlude compensated to some degree for what looked like being another frustrating day.

Alison's mother

That evening, however, saw a possible break-through. While tucking into some excellent fresh fish at a sea-front cafe, Alison's mother, being a friendly person, began chatting to an English couple at the next table. Inevitably, the subject of builders came up and it transpired that the couple had employed an English builder to do some work in a holiday flat they owned. Unfortunately, this was some time ago and they no longer had his details, but his name was Clive and he lived out of town on the road to a nearby village. Directions to the village were scribbled on a paper napkin. Something positive, at last.

By 9 o'clock the following morning, it became obvious that the day was to be another scorcher, so the plan of action was to spend a few hours sitting in the shade with a good book and slices of unbelievably excellent melon, now in season, and a cool glass of juice; the mission to find the English-speaking builder to be postponed until after lunch. Many builders did not work in the afternoons, particularly during the hotter months, preferring to do a few extra hours in the cooler evenings. They had a good chance, therefore, of catching Clive at home during his siesta.

Finding the village, just a group of houses with a bar and small shop, was not a problem. Locating the house proved more difficult. There were no signs on the approaching road of any building company. The only possibility was a modern, not very Spanish-looking bungalow surrounded by a wire security fence behind which a large Rottweiler was stretched out in the shade, panting in the heat.

As they struggled out of the small metal oven that was their car, the Rottweiler sprang alarmingly to life, barking and hurling itself at the wire

53

fence. There was no way they were going to open the gate. Whilst considering their next move, a man appeared at the door to see what all the noise was about, then commanded the dog to be quiet in a gutteral language that they took to be German. Alison had a smattering of schoolgirl French and basic Italian, but no German. Fortunately, the man also had a few words of French. So, in this remote Andalucian village, there ensued a bizarre conversation between a German man and an English woman carried out in pigeon French. Alison was able to discover that Clive did live locally, but the best way to contact him was to visit a certain bar in Motril, where he could be found most nights. Success!

The bar turned out to be one of those gloomy down-at-heel drinking places solely occupied by men, most of whom were smoking. Alison's mother was extremely uncomfortable, but remained grimly supportive as Alison approached the bar and enquired:

"Clive Inglés aqui?" (Clive English here?)

Before the barman could respond, a man sitting at a nearby looked round.

"Who's asking?"

Clive - for it was he - was wearing sandals, khaki shorts and a skimpy vest revealing tattoos from wrists to shoulders. He had a mop of sandy hair and was probably in his mid thirties. Rising to his feet, he asked if he could be of assistance. Assistance being precisely what was required, they quickly filled him in. Immediately grasping the situation, he assured them that he was their man, continuing in his south London accent to enumerate the different jobs he had completed for many satisfied customers, English, Spanish and other nationalities.

He was up to his eyes at the moment but as soon as he could fit it in, he would come and have a "butchers". Could that be tomorrow, they begged, as they were leaving for home in two days? Clive sucked in air through his teeth and tutted a couple of times (demonstrating that he was a proper British builder), before reluctantly agreeing to pay a visit the following evening.

A rendezvous on the road to Los Tablones was agreed so that he could be escorted to the site, and they shook hands and took their leave. Back in the car once again, Alison gave an enormous sigh of relief. They had done it! Not only had they found a builder who could speak English, but one that actually *was* English. The journey to Spain and all the hassles had been worthwhile after all. They headed back to Los Tablones, her mother emphatically saying nothing.

54

When asked why the silence, she explained that she had not taken to Clive at all, expressing her conviction that Clive was "a bit of a geezer"; i.e. not to be trusted.

Despite her mother's qualms, Clive did turn up the following evening at the appointed hour and appeared very relaxed and friendly. Unfortunately, his immediate reaction on arrival at La Caracola was not what Alison wanted to hear.

"Do up this old ruin? You must be joking. You'd be wasting your money, love. Don't even consider it. My advice to you, is knock it down and build a brand new house. I could do that for just about the same money. Maybe even less. Proper foundations, sturdy block walls, decent windows and a proper roof. No messing, eh? Think about it, love."

Alison explained that we liked the idea of living in a traditional old *cortijo* and the last thing we wanted was a modern concrete villa. He argued that the amount of work involved for what we would end up with made no sense at all. Alison's mother was almost certainly on his side but, sensibly, kept her thoughts to herself. Eventually, some measurements were taken and it was agreed that Clive would prepare an estimate for a renovation and another estimate for building a new house. These would be put in the post within the week or so.

Twenty four hours later, Alison and her mother arrived back in England, relieved to have escaped the excessive summer heat of Spain and, in her mother's case, grateful to be safe in her clean and tidy house with rows of reassuring streetlights outside and, inside, absolutely no chance of encountering a passing lizard.

As far as Alison was concerned, it had been five eventful days involving a certain amount of stress interspersed with some very pleasant interludes but, most importantly, job done.

Ten days later, a letter arrived with a Spanish postmark. With great anticipation, we opened the envelope and sat down to study the figures. Our excitement was short lived. Clive's "estimate" for renovation stated that the work would be carried out to a high standard including the installation of kitchen and bathroom. That was it. There was no breakdown of costs whatsoever, merely a total sum. The price given for building a new house of the same size was, not unexpectedly, a little less. Both estimates were many times higher than the amount quoted by our ex-friend Robert.

Impossible. Out of the question. The man had turned out to be the "geezer" Alison's mother had predicted.

There was no time to consider the next move as we both had to fly off to Holland. I was overseeing the installation of a fairly large exhibition for which Alison was researching and writing text, plus sourcing all the photographs for a number of graphic panels.

Strangely enough, it was here, in Rotterdam, that we stumbled across what could possibly be the solution to our building problem in Spain.

CHAPTER ELEVEN
Eddie

We first met Eddie when installing the "Smugglers Adventure" visitor experience in Hastings a year or so before the Rotterdam exhibition. He had been introduced by one of our colleagues as a useful builder cum odd job man who could turn his hand to anything. He was employed in the Hastings caves for a number of weeks to erect blockwork walls, repair cement floors and install various pieces of scenery supplied by a specialist contractor. It turned out that he had no bank account, no driving licence, no permanent address, no P45 or any other documentation to prove who he was. As far as the State was concerned, he did not exist. Consequently, he had to be paid in cash. At nine o'clock in the morning he started work and, with short breaks for tea or a sandwich, he laboured hard and cheerfully until five o'clock in the evening. He only became tetchy if he finished a job and no one could tell him what needed doing next. He hated wasting time.

Muscular, with reddish-brown shoulder length hair in a mullet style – sometimes tied back – plus moustache and beard, you might have taken him for a forty-year-old biker. One imagined there must be a gleaming Harley Davidson parked nearby. The fingers on both of his hands were encrusted with an assortment of rings in all shapes and sizes. We were to discover that he had a ritual with these rings at the end of each working day: after having washed or showered and changed into clean clothes, he would place all the rings on a table and, with a pin, painstakingly clean the day's grit from each one. He would then place the sparkling rings back onto his fingers and, more often than not, take himself off to the pub to spend most of the day's wages. He never drank whilst working but during the evening he could knock back a staggering amount of beer with seemingly no effect.

Setting up the exhibition in Rotterdam required someone dependable to assist with the construction, so Eddie was asked to spend a month or so on site and one evening we found ourselves chatting to him in the hotel bar. We were bemoaning the fact that the people in the City council who were responsible for mounting the event, of which we were only a part, seemed totally disorganised. Alison was having similar trouble with the local museums and art galleries. Photos and information discussed and promised, quite often never materialised.

This discussion about the shortcomings of our Dutch associates inevitably led on to the subject of our unfortunate experience with another Dutchman in

Spain and our subsequent lack of builders. Eddie expressed sympathy and then casually suggested:

"I'll come out and do a bit for you, if you want. Quite fancy a drop of sunshine."

This was an intriguing offer, but would it be practical? There was the cost of flights and accommodation and the fact that we could only be there for short periods. Flights were expensive as this was before the days of budget airlines. Easyjet did not start operating until 1995. On the other hand, at the speed he worked, two weeks of Eddie was equal to four weeks of most other people. So the offer was accepted with arrangements to be made for a fortnight in September 1990, ten weeks later.

On the appointed day, the three of us met at the Gatwick Airport check-in. Eddie was travelling light with only hand luggage in the form of a canvas rucksack, whereas we were carrying large holdalls. As soon as these were handed over, we headed for the departure lounge and the security check. Alison and I were soon through but Eddie was stopped by a Customs Official. The man was delving into the rucksack and we were horrified to see him discover a fearsome looking weapon and brandish it, accusingly, in front of Eddie's face. It was like a hammer with, opposite the head, a long curved chisel. Later we discovered that it was called a Bricklayer's Hammer. What was Eddie thinking – attempting to bring such an implement on to an airplane? In the wrong hands, it could obviously do serious damage. For a while, he and the Customs Official were locked in conversation and then Eddie said something that made them both laugh. The hammer was returned to the rucksack and, to our amazement, the Customs man patted him on the shoulder and waived him on his way. Not for the first time, or the last, we witnessed Eddie using his considerable charm. The only information he would impart by way of explanation was:

"Told him it was a Tool Of My Trade. Had to have it, didn't I? End of story."

When introduced to *La Caracola* the following morning, Eddie was smitten and immediately understood why we had embarked on this project. He soon set to work and although we were not assisting in any of the manual labour, he kept us constantly on the run locating and ferrying an endless supply of materials. His first request was for a cement mixer and a supply of water. We were directed by Roger to go to a street in Motril where lorries were parked waiting for customers. All we had to do was approach one of the drivers and ask for a *cubo de agua* (a container of water) - simple - and provide directions to the *cortijo*. Not so simple.

Undaunted, Alison looked up the Spanish for "Meet on the road to Los Tablones" and "Today or tomorrow?" and "What time?" and we set off. The driver we approached understood what was wanted and where we were to meet but there was confusion about when. He said *"La una"*, which Alison thought was "Monday" and she kept asking "But what time?" and he kept repeating *"La una"*, each time with more emphasis. Eventually he mimed getting into his cab, driving the lorry, getting the water, and driving towards us. Next, he scribed a circle around his watch with a finger, then held up the finger and repeated:

"La una."

The penny dropped. In Spanish *"la una"* (the one) means one o'clock whereas Monday is *lunes.* Another lesson learned and smiles all round.

True to his word, the lorry turned up an hour later carrying a large tank of water. Unfortunately, it was not an enclosed tank, so when the lorry left the tarmac road and climbed up a gradient to our track a great deal of the precious fluid poured from the back of the tank and cascaded onto the ground. The lorry bumped and splashed along the rough track to the *cortijo* and what was left of the water was piped into our *deposito.*

Ordering a cement mixer to be delivered from a builders yard was relatively straightforward, although there was another misunderstanding when Alison asked *"Cuando?"* (When?) and the man answered *"Hoy"*.

Not understanding, she tried *Lunes?* (Monday?), *Martes?* (Tuesday?) and so on, but the man just shook his head and said: *"No. Hoy"*. Getting nowhere, he switched from *"Hoy"* to *"Ahorra"*, and all became clear. Alison just happened to know that *"Ahorra"* meant "Now". Later, we discovered that *"Hoy"* was the word for "Today".

Purchasing the cement *(cemento)* was not a problem but we did have a little embarrassment with the sand. Rather than requesting a bag of sand *(bolsa de arena)*, Alison asked for a *bolsa de arañas* - meaning a bag of spiders!

Eddie was delighted with our efforts. He could now start mixing cement – one of his favourite occupations. The amount of work he could accomplish within a day was truly amazing but he was not very good at planning ahead. He had us driving to and from Motril two and three times a day. He would demand five more bags of cement or two more bags of sand. When we returned, he would need a load of bricks or blocks, which meant organising a delivery. If these did not arrive in time he would switch jobs and it was suddenly vital to have some plastic drainage or water pipes; and when we had found these he would send us back for some special brackets to fix them. We became regular visitors to the builders yards and hardware stores and our pathetic Spanish vocabulary grew to include the words for plaster, fine sand, course sand, bricks, blocks, pipe, wood, nails, screws and glue. On subsequent trips this was later extended to encompass windows, doors, tiles, paint, varnish, wash-basin, sink, bath, taps and toilets.

Alison did nearly all the talking. She was less embarrassed than I at having a go and had recently started attending evening classes back home. Her efforts at trying to make herself understood were generally treated with great tolerance but there was sometimes a difficulty with the men in the building trade, many of whom could not bring themselves to look her in the eye. In this part of Spain, women were still very much "in the kitchen". For example, one never saw a woman driving a car. So when Alison asked a question, quite often the man she was talking to would address the answer to me. A habit that Alison found extremely irritating.

We thought we might have met our Waterloo when Eddie was about to lay a concrete floor and demanded iron reinforcing mesh. He had to have it within the next few hours as the cement mixer was going. We did not understand the logic of this. Surely he could use cement churning around in the mixer for some other job. But no, once Eddie had set himself a task, he became upset if it could not be finished.

Although it was not part of the plan and hardly seemed a priority, while he was in cement mixing mode, Eddie declared that he intended to lay a concrete pad along the front of the house. This, of course, added to the amount of iron mesh required.

Alison looked up the words for iron and mesh and concrete and reinforcing, and armed with the square footage of flooring he was contemplating, which we had to transfer into square metres, we headed once more into town. The man in the builders yard, who had now become quite friendly, directed us to a metal company where we placed our order. The quantity of iron required would certainly not go on the roof rack of our little hire car, so a delivery was arranged for the following morning.

Not being able to hold any sort of conversation with the various suppliers of building materials was quite stressful. No matter how clearly we wrote down our requirements, there would always be supplementary questions. So, to locate and order a quantity of iron mesh and have it delivered the following day, something that would be difficult enough to achieve in England, was a major triumph. But far from being impressed, Eddie' face fell when told that the delivery could not be that afternoon. Heaving a great sigh, he retreated into the house to get on with some other work, leaving us with a sense of failure that we felt was wholly unjustified.

Despite these occasional minor hiccoughs, by the end of Eddie's first two weeks in Spain, the progress in our little *cortijo* was amazing. Cement floors were laid in all the rooms with drainage pipes incorporated in the kitchen and bathroom, and he had bashed through the wall of the kitchen into the donkey house that was to become the bathroom. The drop down into the bathroom was much greater than anticipated and a flight of seven steps had to be created. Sympathetic with our desire for a rustic look, Eddie found several slightly curved olive tree branches to act as lintels for the opening he had created. These he plastered in, leaving the dark wood on view to create a quirky arch. It was so effective that he knocked out some of the stonework above the square doorway from the living room to the kitchen and gave it similar treatment.

Now that the building was cleared of rubbish and every room had a solid floor, it began to look like a proper house at last. *La Caracola* was gradually being brought back to life.

Despite all his hard work, Eddie declared that he had enjoyed the experience and did not hesitate to accept our invitation to repeat the whole process six months later. To avoid any further incidents with H.M. Customs, the Bricklayer's Hammer was left safely in the *cortijo*.

Eddie and Alison surveying the partly laid concrete pad

Opening from kitchen to bathroom

Arch from living room showing olive wood lintel

Arch from kitchen to living room

Window replacing door in bathroom

Eddie relaxing in one of Roger's bedrooms

CHAPTER TWELVE
An Extendable Prostitute

April 1991 saw us back in Los Tablones. On the way from the airport we were very pleased to have Eddie with us when we came to a halt in a tunnel because of what seemed to be a traffic jam. This was rather strange because it was quite late at night and all the vehicles on both sides of the road were lorries, many of them continuously honking their horns. The atmosphere was threatening and the noise was deafening. We waited for some long while but there was no sign of the blockage clearing. I calculated that there was probably just enough room for our small car to drive between the two lines of lorries, so we decided to cautiously ease forward to see if we could get through. All the way through the long tunnel, we ran a gauntlet of hostile looks from the lorry drivers, many of whom were standing beside their vehicles.

Emerging at last into the open, we were forced to halt. Barring our way, deliberately placed across the road, was a burnt-out car. It was surrounded by a sinister-looking group of men, one of whom approached our vehicle. I wound down the window as one of the men began shouting angrily at us, pointing back into the tunnel. I managed to interject with a desperate:

"English. *No comprendo.* English."

The man caught on. *"Ingles, eh?"*

He thought for a while. Then, the road ahead being impassable, he directed us down a side road, indicating that we could go round and eventually rejoin the main road. We thanked him a lot and, mightily relieved, went on our way.

Later, Roger explained that this had been a roadblock by lorry drivers demonstrating against some perceived injustice perpetrated on the area by the local council. It was something to do with the water supply, but he was not aware of the details.

As we were going to be here for a longer period on this trip, we had arranged to stay in Tony's house, *El Cortijuelo*. Eddie got stuck in right away and, true to form, we had difficulty keeping up with his demands for materials.

In the bathroom, the original stable door was filled in, leaving a hole for a window, a further opening was created in an adjacent wall for a second window, and he built a blockwork partition to form a shower cubicle.

When Eddie started knocking stones out of the wall in the gloomy living room to install a window, he discovered that one of the roof beams, seriously chewed by insects, was in danger of collapse. A replacement beam was purchased (another long quest), but Eddie also needed a couple of Acrojacks to hold up the roof while the old beam was removed.

The word for Acrojack did not appear in the Spanish dictionary. We asked Roger and he told us to ask for a *gata*. Either he was mistaken or we misheard, because our request at various builders merchants was met with puzzled looks, sometimes astonishment. We tried adding the word *extensible* (extendable) but this only raised more eyebrows. It was not until much later that we discovered *gata* actually meant 'cat', which unfortunately had another colloquial meaning: prostitute. Small wonder that eyebrows were raised when two foreigners walked into a shop in search of extendable prostitutes. Eventually, wandering around yet another store, we stumbled across what we were looking for and returned in triumph to *La Caracola*.

As soon as measurements could be taken for replacing the four rotting windows plus the brand new window required for the living room, we paid a visit to a specialist carpentry shop and placed our order. They were ready for collection within the week and the frames were all cemented into place a few days later.

All these shopping expeditions required regular trips to the bank for money previously sent out from England. Each time we had to state the reason for drawing out these sums of cash. The answer, reforming a house, would be written down in pencil on a scrap of paper. We imagined that this was, perhaps, some procedure with foreigners to check for money laundering, but we could not imagine what happened to these little scraps of paper. Surely they were not filed. They were always shoved to one side before the money was counted out and our suspicion was that they were binned as soon as we walked out the door.

Eddie was keen to put a cement render on the bathroom walls but this could not be done until all the water pipes were installed. This would require a plumber who, of course, was needed NOW. We pointed out that the chances of finding a plumber who was prepared to drop everything at a moment's notice for a little project in Los Tablones were quite slim, but Eddie merely shrugged and suggested, while we were at it, we might as well engage an electrician. The house was ready for wiring and it would be nice to have lighting and some power points. Electricity was supplied to the *cortijo* by a very dodgy-looking

wire suspended from a nearby pole, but it was not connected to anything inside the house and there was no fuse box or consumer unit.

That evening, we set off on another of what we had come to call our "Quests". Remembering having seen a shop with a sign stating *"Electricista"*, we headed there first. As usual, Alison had prepared her sentences and the man in the shop quickly caught on, indicating that he needed to look at the house by pointing at his eyes and then pointing out through the window. Alison asked him *"Cuando?"* (when?) - a word we had been using a great deal - and in response he said: *"Ahora"* (now) and ushered us out of the shop. We headed back up to Los Tablones with the *electricista* following in his van.

Upon arrival at *La Caracola,* he set about making notes. I had the words in readiness for light fitting, switch and plug socket, so it was soon agreed what had to be done. A tape measure was produced to calculate the wiring runs and there followed a pause while he jotted down prices. Finally, he wrote a figure on his note pad, tore off the page and handed it over, saying: *"Todo"* (everything) - another one of those words constantly used when shopping, or rather, when finishing shopping. The price was far less than anticipated so we indicated our acceptance before asking once again: *"Cuando"?* To our astonishment, the reply was:

"Mañana."

Before he was allowed to leave, we showed him the bathroom with its lack of *tubos* (pipes). He caught on immediately, saying a sentence that included the words *amigo* and *fontanero* (which we now knew was a plumber) and, again, *mañana*. We were becoming fans of this *electricista*.

During the next three days *La Caracola* did not know what had hit it. Three *electricistas* up and down ladders fixing cables in yellow plastic tubing along the ceiling and down the walls, and two *fontaneros* cutting, bending and fitting copper pipes. The price for the plumbing, including a serious amount of copper, was ridiculously cheap, and it was all completed with such good humour.

Unfortunately, fate decreed that I should miss most of the installation. I have a history of back problems and, following a very uncomfortable night, I found myself unable to stand or walk without pain and sitting was worse. Alison took me to the hospital in Motril where, after a perfunctory examination, they took an X-ray of the lower spine and concluded that it was a strained ligament. It would recover, the specialist declared, with one or two weeks of bed-rest. This I knew to be a false diagnosis having experienced identical symptoms in the past.

It was out of the question to endure such discomfort for the remainder of our stay and Alison was not surprised when I stated my intention of returning to London to see my chiropractor. Trying to make an appointment from an open call box in a noisy street in Motril was not easy. Informed that no appointments were available for several days, Alison explained that she was calling from Spain and her husband, in great pain, was flying back in the morning specifically to be seen. Under the circumstances, they agreed to fit me in. Another phone call was then necessary to book a flight. Fortunately, there was a seat available.

For the journey to the airport, the back seats were folded down in the hired hatchback so that I could lie down on some folded blankets. I hobbled through Customs and stood around in the departure lounge waiting for the flight call, as it was too painful to sit down. The three hour plane journey was a nightmare as I had to be seated most of the time. Our car was parked at Gatwick Airport and somehow I managed to drive it to the houseboat on Taggs Island where I rested until it was time for some serious vertebrae manipulation.

My chiropractor smiled when I sidled into his consulting room.

"What have you been up to this time?"

Apart from sleeping on a sagging bed and having every muscle in the body as taught as bowstrings due to the stress of trying to restore a ruin in Spain, nothing really. He told me to stand in front of him, facing away, and sway gently side to side from the hips. He then touched a point on my lower spine.

"That's the spot, isn't it?"

"Ouch! Yes."

It had taken him a few seconds to diagnose the problem where two hours at the Spanish hospital with a physical examination and X-Rays had failed. Ten minutes later, after rubbing in some oil to soothe the inflamed muscles, my body was twisted in various directions and with a sudden forceful downward pressure on the spine, the offending vertebrate was clicked back into place. I was sent on my way and although very sore, the excruciating pain had gone. Hopefully, not to return.

Feeling much better after a blissfully restful night, I returned to Gatwick airport and by mid afternoon was once again basking in the warm sunshine of

In the shower

Andalucia. Alison was waiting at Malaga airport with the news that we were now the proud owners of a number of switches and plug sockets. Even more exciting, a little electric water pump had been fitted in the *deposito*. And if I wished to see all the copper pipework in the bathroom, I would have to hurry, as Eddie was about to smother them all with cement.

Before the electricity could be switched on we needed a *contador* (meter box) and this had to be supplied and fitted by the local electricity company. So, next morning it was business as usual and on to the next Quest. The electricity office in Motril, incredibly hot and airless, was full of waiting customers all of whom had to discuss their problems at length with the two officials, one man and one woman, seated behind separate desks. Half an hour or so went by, then the woman staff member stood up and, without a word, walked to the door and out into the street. Apparently, it was coffee time. When she returned some fifteen minutes later, her colleague promptly rose and left the building. By this time, we could have done with coffees ourselves. Eventually, it was our turn and Alison explained our need for a *contador,* giving the woman a piece of paper with our personal details and whereabouts of the *cortijo.* As proof of ownership, we had also brought along the sale agreement. She glanced at this and then asked for our *escritura de propiedad.* We made her understand that there was no *escritura.* We were waiting for the *abogado* to sort this out. She shook her head and explained something that included the words *ayuntamiento* (town hall) and *papel* (paper) and *necesario* (necessary). Alison tried to clarify the situation by asking in her best Spanish:

"Vamos a el ayuntamiento?" (We go to the town hall?)

"Si."

"Que es este papel?" (What is this paper?)

For an answer, she wrote some words on a sheet of headed paper, handed it over and waved us vaguely in the direction of the *ayuntamiento.*

Grappling with bureaucracy with no proper grasp of the language is an exhausting business. So, before facing the civil servants in the town hall, what was urgently required – in fact, *necesario* - was a strong restorative coffee. Throughout Spain the coffee is always a treat, tasting like real coffee. Most importantly, it is served in proper cups, unlike the bitter stuff that comes in cardboard vats at three or four times the price in the UK.

At the *ayuntamiento,* the receptionist studied our piece of paper and directed us to a room on the second floor. Here, there were several people sitting behind desks working away in silence. Nobody acknowledged our presence as we entered the room, so we stood in the doorway for a while, hoping that one of them would look up. Nobody did, so we approached the least scary looking official, a young woman busy writing something behind a stack of files. She looked up.

"Si?"

Alison, forcing a smile, opened with a cheery *"Buenas dias"* and presented the piece of paper, adding the words *contador por nuestra casa* (meter for our house). The woman glanced at it briefly and then asked for our *escritura.* We then went through the whole rigmarole of showing the purchase agreement and explaining that the *abogado* would have the *escritura* in the future. All this took a little while because of the language difficulties with many a *"no comprendo"* on our part. There followed questions about the *cortijo*. Again we did not understand and, to be helpful, Alison said *"reforma"*, being the word used for making improvements to a building. This provoked a strong reaction and an emphatic speech culminating in our paperwork being thrust back at us.

Alison looked shocked. Having grasped a sufficient number of words to understand the gist of what the woman had said, she explained it to me.

"I think she's saying we can't have permission for electricity because we are not allowed to reform the house without planning permission."

"Not allowed to reform? Does that mean everything we have done is illegal?"

"I suppose it does."

"Bloody hell! So what happens next? Do we have to stop the work?"

"We need to get planning permission."

"Yes, and how many weeks or months is that going to take?"

We decided the best strategy was to play dumb and say *"no comprendo"*. This we continued to repeat every time she tried to get through to us using simpler language. As her voice rose in frustration, the interchange sparked some interest in the rest of the room. A man from an inner office, perhaps a senior official, sauntered across to see what all the fuss was about and when informed of our crime, enquired the whereabouts of the *cortijo*. Upon learning that it was in Los Tablones, he pulled a wry face, saying dismissively "Los Tablones!" followed by what we gathered was something along the lines of "That scrubby little place in the hills. Don't waste your time. Let them have what they want."

Frustrated and aggrieved, the woman was about to argue when he turned his back and strode away. The man had spoken and that was that. On this occasion, we were happy to overlook this country's unacceptable macho culture.

A few minutes later we were back out on the street clutching the precious *papel* the woman had grudgingly prepared and stamped several times. It had been handed over with bad grace, but we did not care. The crisis was averted.

71

The electricity office was full to bursting upon our return and being somewhat traumatized by recent events, we lacked the will to face another long wait. Instead, we back travelled into town early the following morning before it became too busy. Forms were signed, fees were paid and a date agreed for fitting our *contador*.

While in Motril so early in the day, we took the opportunity to set about our next Quest. Being aware that the windows of local houses were all fitted with security grilles, many quite ornate, we thought it probably wise to follow suit. There were several metal workshops in the town and one of these was selected at random. Alison produced our list of grilles, explaining that we departed for England in ten days. No problem, we were told. You can have them in two days. True to their word, two days later they were ready for collection.

So much had been achieved in our little house by the time we packed up to leave. We now had five windows with brand new frames and shutters, all with security grilles. We had electricity and, wonder of wonders, there was water issuing from our taps, although installing the sink, basin, shower, bath and toilet would have to wait until next time.

The completion of the project seemed tantalizingly close. We were not to know that because of a series of events in England, both good and bad, it would be a year and a half before we could return to *La Caracola*.

CHAPTER THIRTEEN
Fireworks

A period of small and not very lucrative design jobs coupled with commissions for two large and time consuming projects that, for one reason or another never saw the light of day, kept us busy for many months with not a lot of income. Alison's one-woman shows were proving popular, but after paying travel and sometimes hotel expenses for herself and a technician who handled the lighting and sound, there was not a great deal of profit. Not for the first time, we questioned the logic of sinking money into a property we seldom visited. The cost of taking Eddie to Spain was out of the question and it seemed pointless to go there on our own. That is, until Alison and I made our momentous decision.

On the 31st October 1992 we were married. It was a low budget but extremely joyous affair. Official business at the Registry Office in Kingston-Upon-Thames was followed by champagne on the houseboat with close members of the family, including my three sons, Mark, Dominic and Robin. We then repaired to Alison's family home in Redhill where her parents had laid on a splendid buffet-style supper for a group of our best friends. Alison's older brother had made a brilliant cake, expertly iced, so our only expense was for the wine. The one extravagance was the purchase of more than a hundred pounds-worth of impressively large fireworks. You got an impressive selection for your money in those days. These were set out in the not very large garden by friend and colleague Roger Straker, who handled all the technical side of our exhibitions. Seeing the size of some of the set pieces and the cardboard tubes being buried in the ground for the mortars, Alison's father expressed concern about the safety of his trees and his brand new garden chalet. Roger assured him that there was absolutely no danger, despite the labels warning that the audience should stand at least sixty feet back, whereas the space available meant that the happy wedding party would never be more than thirty feet away. It was a truly splendid pyrotechnical display. Some people were surprised, but nobody was hurt.

The discussion about where to spend the honeymoon was brief. Both of us wanted to visit our little *cortijo*. We only had to find money for the airfares and the cost of hiring a car in Spain. Accommodation at *El Cortijuelo* was free, thanks once again to our generous friends.

It was meant to be ten days of relaxation, but we could not resist making improvements to our *cortijo*. The main achievement was to have our ceilings plastered. Tony had told us of some brothers living in Los Tablones who did this kind of work. Once located, we indicated that we had ceilings needing their attention and they immediately accompanied us to *La Caracola*. Quickly sizing up the job, they seemed happy to do the work and mentioned a price in pesetas. Alison by now had a pretty good grasp on numbers and as it was very little money, immediately agreed. Then one of the men said to me: *Nombre?*

I had no idea what he was asking. Alison thought he wanted our English telephone number and wrote it down on a piece of paper, which the man declined, repeating: *Nombre. Nombre.*

Whatever they wanted seemed important, so we had the bright idea of consulting Roger. Beckoning the men to follow us to *el hombre ingles - habla español* (the Englishman - he speaks Spanish), we set off down the hill. Roger could not believe what we were asking him to translate after all our time spent in Spain. He heaved a great sigh and cast his eyes to heaven, then explained that all the men wanted to know was our <u>name</u>.

There followed a conversation in Spanish with a great deal of laughter, no doubt at our expense. Nevertheless, everything was sorted out and the brothers arrived the following morning. The ceilings were all plastered beautifully the same day.

We had noticed that water was seeping through the walls of the *deposito* in a few places and Roger's advice was to coat the inside with a weak solution of cement. Alison immediately volunteered for the job. Once she had clambered down through the hatch, I handed her a bucket of cement and a distemper brush and left her to it. Every so often a distant echoey cry was heard which meant that the cement needed replenishing. More buckets were handed down until the whole process was completed. I felt a little guilty leaving her in there for so long, but she  said that it was very peaceful. Lovely and cool. In fact, quite enjoyable. Added to which, who else could claim to have spent their honeymoon inside a large concrete water tank?

While this was going on, I made a start on giving a good dowsing of anti-insect treatment to the roof beams and the windows. All this woodwork was then varnished a dark walnut colour. The plaster on the ceilings did not take long to dry and we were able to apply a couple of coats of white paint. Before our eyes, *La Caracola* was beginning to transform from a desolate ruin into a cosy little house.

When dealing with the *ayuntamiento*, the electricity company, banks or any other official body, we were continually being asked for our NIE *(Número de Identidad de Extranjero)*. This is required by any foreigner starting a business or buying property and is generally useful for identification. Spanish nationals all carry a DNI (documento nacional de identidad), similar to the compulsory Identity Card issued during World War Two in the UK. The DNI is a plastic card with one's photo, address and personal details and, of course, a number. This little card avoids the nonsense of having to present an assortment of bank statements and household bills for identification when dealing with any form of bureaucracy in Britain.

To obtain our NIEs, it was necessary to present ourselves at the police station twice, once with our passports to fill in an application form and the second time to collect it. On both occasions, of course, there was a great deal of hanging around because there was only one person dealing with these requests.

The Andalucians appear resigned to long waits wherever officialdom is involved, particularly in banks. Every transaction is accompanied by what we would consider a great deal of unnecessary discussion, but nobody seems to mind. They have a system to avoid queuing; a person entering will ask *Quién es el ultimo?* (who is the last?). On being informed, they take a seat if one is available and just keep an eye on that individual. Most places have chairs dotted around for the elderly and infirm, although seldom enough.

Towards the end of our honeymoon, there was a memorable day was when we drove to Granada, only an hour away, to visited the Alhambra. This is the most fantastic palace/fortress built by the Moors who came from Morocco in 711AD and went on to rule most of Spain for eight hundred years.

We had been warned to ignore the gypsies who stood on the steep road up to the Alhambra, urgently signaling tourists to stop and park, then requesting payment to look after the cars. The wretched innocents who were caught, then faced an extremely long climb to the top of the hill where there is an enormous car park conveniently situated beside the entrance to the palace.

The Alhambra is a collection of large, mostly square buildings, the interiors of which are decorated with tile mosaics in complicated mathematical patterns, incredibly ornate carved stucco and painted wooden ceilings. Outside there are courtyards with arcades, columns and fountains, and the beautiful gardens have been designed for the hot climate with shaded arbours and running water.

Our only mistake was not to take advantage of the restaurants in the street before starting the tour. There is no opportunity to purchase food in the Alhambra and by the time we had completed our tour, we were famished and extremely thirsty from the midday sun. On a subsequent visit a few years later, we made sure to eat first and carry bottles of water with us.

The holiday was over all too quickly. Although much progress had been made, it was now three years since *La Caracola* had come into our lives and there was still a depressing amount of work to be done. We were determined to get Eddie out again as soon as possible.

Before leaving, we checked with our *abogado*, Juan Alvarez, to see if there was news of the *escritura*. He had heard nothing but was not concerned, reiterating that these things take time. Although he may not have been concerned, our investment in the property was growing with each visit and we still had no watertight proof of ownership. What if some distant relation of the seller did pop up out of the woodwork to claim his inheritance? Robert's original estimate for renovation had been far exceeded, partly due to subcontracting the plumbing and electrics and partly because of Eddie's airfares and daily rate which, by no means excessive by British standards, was more than the locals would charge. One could not help worrying about those wretched chickens that we were still counting.

CHAPTER FOURTEEN
Eddie Again

April 1993 and we were staying once again in Tony and Monique's *El Cortijuelo*. It had been two years since Eddie's last visit and we were soon back in the old routine. Every morning, before we were up and about, Eddie would be in the kitchen making himself a breakfast of bread and marmalade with a large mug of tea. On most days, he set off for work before we emerged and by the time we arrived at the *cortijo* there was inevitably something vital required from Motril. So off we would go on another Quest. For his midday meal, Alison always made two sandwiches from freshly baked long crispy loaves bought in the town. These were filled with an assortment of goodies such as ham, cheeses, grapes, olives, avocados, lettuce, etc. The cans of beer we originally offered were rejected. He did, however, require large quantities of drinking water. Then, in the evening, after showering, changing into clean clothes and completing the cleaning of the rings, he would wish to be taken to a bar for beer and *tapas*. To his surprise and delight, he found that every time he ordered a beer it came with a small saucer of *tapas*, it being the law in the Granada region of Andalucia to avoid drunkenness. The bars all have a variety of *tapas* dishes on the go, so with one beer you might be served with fish, then with successive beers they could be based on pork, goat or some other meat. Most of them delicious.

Before his first trip to a bar, we had given him the word for beer *(cervesa)* and when ordering his first, the barman enquired: *"Chica?"* and Eddie, thinking this was possibly a brand of beer, nodded. Looking forward to quaffing a decent pint, he was disgusted when what he called "a smear" arrived in a wine glass. In Spanish, *chica* literally means "girl" but colloquially the word is used to denote a small glass of beer. Later, when he discovered that a proper sized beer comes in a *tubo,* he was in turns amused and mortified to think that he had been ordering "girlie drinks" all evening. A *tubo* equates to what we would call a tumbler - so still not very large - but unlike many Brits, the Spanish do not feel it necessary to drink vast quantities of alcohol and we have never witnessed drunken or rowdy behaviour in all the years of visiting the south of Spain.

As Alison never touches alcohol and I am not a pub person, we did not accompany Eddie on his drinking sessions. He was very happy to be dropped off and then collected at a prearranged time, usually after about two hours. Although he spoke no word of Spanish, such was his personality that when we

77

arrived to pick him up, he would inevitably be holding court with a group of locals. They would be jabbering away in Spanish, he would be speaking in English, and they would all be laughing. One evening, we delivered him to a small bar-restaurant in a nearby village, arranging to return in two hours. At the appointed time we found him seated at a table with three Englishmen who lived and worked locally. They were obviously enjoying each other's company and Eddie asked if we could come back in an hour or so. No problem. An hour later, there were many empty *tubos* on the table and the conversation had become a little more raucous. They were all having a good time so, once again, Eddie requested an extra hour. Fortunately, it was less than a ten-minute journey so we were not too bothered. Returning to the bar a third time, we found Eddie, bright as a button, but the other three very much the worse for wear. One was slumped on the table asleep, one was sitting back in his chair staring glassy-eyed into the distance, while the other was desperately trying to continue the conversation but having trouble formulating the words. Seeing us at the door, Eddie rose to his feet, smiling cheerily.

"Sorry to break up the party, guys. Good fun. See you again sometime, eh?"

With that, he walked briskly out of the bar, showing no sign of any alcohol having passed his lips. Sinking happily into the back seat of the car, he summed up the evening.

"That was a good session. Interesting blokes, but they can't hold their drink."

On another evening, Alison noticed Eddie sitting in the kitchen engrossed in a book. Being an avid reader herself and acquainted with that particular book, they got talking about their favourite novels. It turned out that he was remarkably well read and his impressive knowledge of literature stood him in good stead as a member of the quiz team in his local pub. The man was full of surprises.

Work at *La Caracola* continued apace. I happened to mention that one day it would be good to build a little store room down at the lower end of the house against the *deposito*. It would be useful for tools, paints, brushes, etc. "Excellent idea" said Eddie and promptly started to prepare the ground for a concrete base. Within three days, in between other jobs, he had completed a splendid store incorporating the old window from the kitchen and the door from the donkey house.

Meanwhile, floor tiles were laid in the kitchen in a pleasing diagonal pattern. This was more time consuming than laying them square, but Eddie insisted it would look much better. And so it did. We were determined to have the traditional warm red clay tiles that were standard in all the old *cortijos*. However, a request for these rough unglazed *lozas* in Motril's smart tile shops got us nowhere. They either looked completely blank, or became very sniffy at the very idea of stocking such an item. Fortunately, our friend in the builders yard was able to direct us to a dingy little tile store in one of the back streets. The 30cm x 30cm tiles cost the equivalent of 20p each - and they looked stunning. The only down side was their absorbency. So once they were laid, we soaked them with a water sealant for protection against staining. Unfortunately, the two large tins of sealant we tried to bring out on the airplane were impounded as being dangerous chemicals, but our ever-helpful friends, Tony and Monique, brought some from Paris the next time they drove down.

As soon as the walls in the kitchen were given a cement coating, Eddie built a work top with brick supports rendered with cement. The surface, which I later tiled, was made of 1m x 2m slabs of terracotta about 3cm thick that locked together. A similar unit on the other side of the room housed the cooker.

In the bathroom, laid with white floor tiles, Eddie built another surface for the washbasin. We had already ordered the sink, basin, bath and shower unit and once they were installed our *fontanero* friends came to plumb them all in. At the same time, they supplied and fitted a butane gas water heater.

Before the heater could be installed in a recess at the bottom of the steps to the bathroom, the walls needed a cement render before painting. Alison, who was very much smaller than Eddie, offered to do this job. He dismissed the suggestion, saying that he would not want her to work in such a small airless space. Alison argued that it was only cement render. It would not kill her. Eddie, looking a little embarrassed, explained that the render had a "secret ingredient" to make it easier to work with, and the "secret ingredient" was a bit unpleasant. Alison knew from her work as an historical researcher that this "secret ingredient" was ammonia. Builders had been employing it as a stabilizer since medieval times. To Eddie's surprise, she declared:

"What you are trying to say is that you've peed in it. Of course. What's the problem?"

A big grin spread across Eddie's face as he handed her the brush and the bucket of render. Within half an hour she had completed the job and, in Eddie's eyes, had gained a great number of brownie points.

The gas bottles we had to purchase ourselves, and it was a curious process that involved visiting an official office in Motril to obtain a licence. We had to show them our NIE documents, state our address (not that *La Caracola, Los Tablones* meant anything to anybody) and then say whether we wanted one or two bottles. Forms were filled in with all the details, copies were made and then stamped many times. A fairly large fee was requested and, once paid, a copy of the licence was handed over. We then asked for our two bottles of gas and the man looked slightly offended. They did not sell gas bottles - the very idea! Fortunately, Alison knew an important word that was often required meaning "where?".

"Donde?"

Perfectly aware that we spoke no Spanish, he rattled off some directions that were impossible to follow. Asked to repeat them, we were none the wiser. The man was determined to be unhelpful and obviously wished to be rid of us, so we called it a day and determined to ask Roger.

The purchasing of gas bottles, for reasons we could never fathom, turned out to be a clandestine affair. On certain days of the week a small lorry laden with bottles would be parked up a side street, round a corner on a piece of rough ground, well out of sight of the main road. When you drew up, a small, square, shabby-looking elderly man climbed out of the cab and hoiked the bottles off the lorry. We had brought along our licence to prove that we were bona fide customers but he waived this away (most likely unable to read) muttering the price in a hoarse whisper. In silence, the required amount of pesetas was handed over and he lifted a bottle into the boot of the car. We drove away with the uneasy feeling that at any moment we might be apprehended by the *Guardia Civil* for carrying an illegal substance. On subsequent occasions when the gas ran out, the empty bottle was exchanged for a full one, paying however many pesetas the old fellow decided was the going rate for that particular week.

It was around this time that we received an unexpected bonus when Roger discovered that water from his swimming pool was leaking into the plant room below. He was removing all the tiles and replacing them with a special water-proof epoxy paint. Consequently, he had a large pile of perfectly good blue tiles going spare and we were offered to take our pick. They needed cleaning and I spent a couple of happy hours in the sunshine with a bucket of caustic soda, a scrubbing brush and some rubber gloves removing the old cement. Later, I fixed them to the walls of the bathroom where they looked splendid.

There were other uses for caustic soda. Roger's houses were full of wooden items such as lamp stands, tables, cupboards and charming wooden plate racks. These had all been stripped of old paint and varnish by soaking them in a tank of caustic soda; the tank being simply constructed with a large piece of plastic draped over rows of cement blocks forming a square.

We had found a door, dumped by the side of the road, that would be ideal for the gas heater recess and Roger had donated some decorative mouldings that might find a place in *La Caracola,* so we set about building our own tank. Caustic soda is pernicious stuff that can cause severe burns if in contact with the skin, but we had no trouble finding a shop in Motril where we could purchase several large containers of the stuff.

Wearing protective rubber gloves, we carefully slid the door into the tank and almost immediately the thick brown paint began to blister and bubble. Left for twenty minutes or so, the paint became a thick goo that could be wiped off with a floor mop revealing the beautifully grained timber. Hosed, scrubbed down with water and given two coats of linseed oil it looked as good as new and far superior to anything we could have bought in a shop. Eddie constructed a frame for the door, and the heater recess became an attractive cupboard.

Although we now had running water, thanks to the little pump in the *deposito*, the lavatory could not be used without a septic tank. Once again, Roger was consulted. The answer was to build an enclosed concrete box about a metre square and 80 centimetres high with the soil pipe entering high up on one side, and a smaller drainage pipe low down on the other side. The tank should be built some fifteen metres or so down the hill away from the house. That was it, apart from buying a special powder to flush down the toilet every once in a while. This product contained micro-organisms and enzymes to digest the waste. We wondered what would happen if and when this enclosed tank became full. Simple, we were told. Just get some dynamite, blow it off the hillside and build another. In a funny sort of way, we were quite looking forward to that day. Sadly, it never came.

Standing on my "Poo Hut"

In no time, Eddie had constructed what we were now calling our "Poo Hut" and run in the pipes. There was a similar septic tank at *El Cortijuelo* and we borrowed some of Tony's special powder containing the micro-organisms and poured these "Poo Beetles" down our lavatory. Job done.

To avoid flooding the Poo Hut, Eddie arranged that the grey water from washing and showering was piped out onto the land to water the shrubs or trees, should we ever get round to planting any. We now had running hot and cold water and a working loo. Surely, one more push and we would be bringing in the furniture.

During a celebratory meal in Motril on our final evening, plans were discussed for the next visit. In the living room and bedroom, floor tiles had to be laid and the walls rendered. A new front door was needed plus a door to the bathroom. Eddie reckoned that all this could be achieved in two to three weeks.

There were still some walls and surfaces to be tiled and a good deal of painting, but this was something Alison and I could handle.

What none of us knew at the time, was that Eddie would never return.

CHAPTER FIFTEEN
Fernando

Later that year, having decided that our next "holiday" would be in October, we tried to get hold of Eddie. Not having any permanent address, contact was normally made through certain members of the staff at the Smugglers Adventure in Hastings with whom Eddie kept in touch. On this occasion we were distressed to learn that he had been taken seriously ill while on a visit to Holland. Not much was known except that he had collapsed and been rushed to hospital with what was thought to be a problem with his liver. Presumably, all those years of drinking had finally caught up with him. We asked to be kept informed of any further news. Meanwhile, we were once again without a builder.

What to do? This time it was our friend Tony who came to the rescue. He was employing a local builder called Fernando at *El Cortijuelo* to construct a wall around part of his land. The job would soon be completed and Fernando was willing to give us a couple of weeks in November. We asked Tony to sign him up immediately.

Our third builder had the looks of a film star. Slim, average height, black hair, watery blue eyes and eyelashes any girl would die for. Fernando had also done some work for Roger and when Alison remarked that she was enjoying having a dishy man about the house (I did not take offence), Roger looked uneasy and warned her very seriously to watch out for the wife.

Fernando

"As soon as she realises there is a woman around, she will be up there. Mark my word. She is insanely jealous. He is not allowed to move without her say-so. I tell you, that woman is a WITCH!"

Roger was so vehement on the subject that one wondered whether he had fallen foul of The Witch himself.

All went well at the beginning. Fernando rendered the outside walls of the house with cement and fitted a new front door. He then laid *lozas* on the floor of the bedroom.

As predicted, The Witch did turn up for no particular reason we could see; but as we were not able to engage in any conversation, the visit might well have been completely innocent. An attractive enough woman about the same age as Fernando, she spoke a few words to her husband and took a brief look around the house. Passing us on the way out, she muttered the obligatory *Hasta luego* (until the next time) and departed. Hopefully, she had decided that Alison was not a threat.

Although Fernando worked nowhere near as rapidly as Eddie and the finishes were not quite as good, we were satisfied with the progress. He also kept us amused by a strange affectation involving T-shirts. He would turn up each morning wearing jeans, shirt and baseball cap, carrying a plastic bag containing his lunch and other necessities. More often than not, he would appear a little later with a coloured - say red - T-shirt tied like a turban around his head. Later in the day this might well be exchanged for a blue T-shirt. We were intrigued to know the thinking behind this use of T-shirt headgear and why it was necessary to change to a new one every few hours. Perhaps it kept him cool. Perhaps it kept his beautiful hair clean. We did not enquire.

Our disappointment with Fernando was on the penultimate day of his two weeks. He had laid *lozas* in the living room and grouted them with cement and, as was the practice, he was neatly smoothing off the grout with bundles of damp horse hair. It would only take him a matter of fifteen minutes or so to finish the job, but he kept looking anxiously at his watch. Suddenly, he stopped what he was doing, grabbed his plastic bag and said he was leaving. We tried to object, indicating the grouting that was still rough and would soon dry that way. He insisted that it was not a problem, he would clean it off tomorrow.

"Es importante que ahora voy." (It is important that I go now).

Then, by way of explanation, he said: *"me mujer, me mujer"* (my woman, my woman) and legged it down the track.

The Witch! Roger had warned us.

Fernando never did manage to smooth off the grout. There were a number of other jobs to complete on his final day and time ran out. When we eventually did move into the house, Alison spent several evenings crawling around the floor with hammer and bolster smashing off lumps of cement sticking up between the tiles.

That was the last we ever saw of Fernando. Before we returned to Spain the next time, he had left the area. Roger said it was because his wife had delusions of grandeur. The people in Los Tablones were not good enough for *Madam*. She *made* him move to the town. *The Witch!*

By now Roger had a new partner helping to run the holiday business. Pepe was a shy, amiable Spaniard with a quiet sense of humour who was an excellent foil to Roger's more gregarious and artistic temperament. Apart from organising the shopping and cooking the food, he had useful gardening skills, having been brought up in *el campo* (the countryside). Unfortunately for us, he spoke not a word of English and even when he did try us with some simple Spanish phrases, it was difficult to understand because of his Andalucian accent.

Roger had some very surprising news of his former partner, Robert. Apparently, he had met and married a French woman and was now living in Paris. Hopefully, the parting from his former lover had been amicable and Miguel was now back in Motril taking care of his wife and six children. Funny old world!

A major event took place at *La Caracola* - the boiling of our first kettle. We had bought a Calor gas oven and an electric fridge, so cups of tea and coffee were now available for the workers with fresh milk from the fridge. Suddenly, life became more civilized.

Before departing once more for the UK, without much optimism we knocked on the door of Juan Alvarez, *Abogado*. Did he have any news on our *escritura*? His welcoming smile turned into a pained expression, as though we were questioning his professional integrity. Of course he had the *escritura*. It was in our file. He had been waiting for us to collect it.

He called for his secretary to bring in the file and, extracting the precious document, handed it over. Rather disappointingly, it was just a few typed paragraphs on a couple of sheets of paper with a lot of official date stamps in several colours. However, it did have our names and London address, so it was presumably all that was required. We paid him a fee for his work, shook his well-manicured hand, expressed our thanks, and said farewell.

Precisely six years had passed since we had concluded that dodgy deal in Paco's Bar. Six long years of uncertainty. Now we were unquestionably the rightful owners of *La Caracola* and half a hillside in Spain. But the house was still unfinished. We could not live in it and, once again, we were without a builder.

CHAPTER SIXTEEN
Pepe

As luck would have it, Tony and Monique had been introduced to a Spanish couple from Los Tablones who were looking for work. They engaged Pepe to water their cactus garden and trees once a week and his wife to occasionally air the house and have it cleaned and ready for their arrival. Although Pepe advertised himself as a gardener, work was sparse and he was more than happy to turn his hand to whatever was on offer. Tony soon had him laying paving on his terraces and doing general maintenance jobs.

Pepe was warned that his address had been given to some English friends who needed some work done at their *cortijo*, so he was not surprised when, in March 1996, we knocked on his door and introduced ourselves. Alison had now completed two years of evening classes but her Spanish was still extremely basic. The lessons mostly consisted of learning sentences like: "My hotel does not have a sea view." and "Can I have a salad with my fish?". Not very useful when trying to negotiate a deal with a builder.

Pepe, the fourth builder on our little project, was short, roundly tubby, perhaps in his early thirties, with black curly hair and a small moustache. He liked to talk and, although he must have known it was pointless, persisted on initiating conversations, perhaps in the hope that if he talked at us enough something would eventually rub off.

Although he was working for someone else at the time, he managed to fit in a few jobs for us. These included the construction of shelving and a wardrobe spanning one entire wall of the bedroom. At last we had ample "his and hers" hanging space. Pepe also fitted a bathroom door and two more doors for the recess above the end of the bath.

This was only a short visit to do some decorating and to collect a few items of furniture we had shipped out from England to an agent in Fuengirola, a few miles the other side of Malaga. Included in the shipment were a bed, dining table and chairs, two cane easy chairs and a small cane sofa, plus a few boxes containing items such as bed linen and crockery. Having hired a van in Nerja, we telephoned the agent, an Englishman, to say we were coming that evening. For some reason, he tried to put us off. The road to Malaga, he said, was impassable because of landslips from the recent rain. We knew this to be unlikely as we had driven that way only the day before, so we said that we were coming anyway and would be there by 5.00 o'clock. The directions he gave us were simple. It was a matter of turning left at the second roundabout into the town – he gave us the name of the street - then take the third right. We would see the company's sign outside the building. It could not be missed.

As anticipated, there were no problems with landslips and we found ourselves approaching Fuengirola well before the appointed hour. There were several roundabouts both before and into the town and none of the streets had nameplates. What to do? We did not have a mobile phone in those days, so it was a matter of retracing our steps and trying every one. We drove round the streets for half an hour or more, becoming more and more frustrated. Then Alison suggested driving into the town to find a public telephone. This took a while and by the time she was ringing the number, we were already half an hour late. There was no reply, just a recorded invitation to leave a message. Had the man gone home? Alison's message was not over-polite.

I was all for calling it a day, but Alison suggested a final tour of the area where we had seen a number of warehouses. By pure chance, when driving down yet another unnamed street, we spied the company sign on one of the buildings. A large furniture van with a British number plate was parked outside and when we pulled up, the driver jumped down from the cab and enquired in a cheery East London voice if we were the people who had been ringing. This splendid fellow had heard Alison's phone message while he was unloading, but was unable to answer because the telephone was in a locked office. The boss had, as we suspected, bunked off. Out of the goodness of his heart, the man had waited around just in case we did manage to locate the place. He opened up the loading door and helped carry our furniture and boxes to the van. Then, shrugging off our effusive thanks, wished us luck and climbed back into his cab and drove off.

Soil arriving to create a field

The other reason for this trip to Spain was to investigate the possibility of a permanent water supply. During the past few years, we had witnessed large areas of land being flattened by bulldozers followed by loads of topsoil brought in and spread on the rocky ground. Olive trees that had been standing for hundreds of years were uprooted and burnt. This previously arid land was becoming fertile, made possible by a government-sponsored programme of irrigation largely funded by the EU. Spain had joined the European Community in 1986, which became the European Union in 1993.

Massive water pipes, coloured dark red, could now be seen snaking up and down the hills from newly created reservoirs. Pumping stations were constructed to pump water up the sides of valleys. The owners of what had been worthless land, now living and working in the towns, began to make serious money from growing fruit and vegetables. And once all the accessible stretches of land had been flattened, they started carving great terraces out of the hillsides.

Sadly for us, not only was our wonderful vista of olive trees amongst the rocks, bracken and thyme fast disappearing, but the farmers started erecting enormous metal frames covered in plastic sheeting known as *invernaderas plásticas* (plastic greenhouses). With the constant sunshine in southern Spain, these ugly blots on the landscape were capable of producing tomatoes, melons, and other fruit all year round. The forced tomatoes were totally tasteless compared with the delicious sun-ripened tomatoes available in the Motril market, but they were big and round and red and mostly for export.

Once a landowner had hired a bulldozer, the object was to flatten as much land as possible just in case it might be useful in the future. One day we were horrified to see one of these machines deliberately destroying the Roman viaduct on the other side of the valley. This criminal act was simply to gain a few metres of land along the bottom of the *barranco*. To make matters worse, it then went on to attack the Roman tower, repeatedly bashing at the walls until half of the building came crashing down. This mindless vandalism, creating a sorry ruin of an extraordinary piece of history, turned out to be for no purpose whatsoever. The land was never used for cultivation.

Roger was so incensed, he determined to report this outrage to the Mayor of Motril who happened to be an acquaintance. The Mayor was invited for coffee and then taken along to see the devastation. Completely unaware of the significance of the site, he was genuinely interested to learn that it had been built by the Romans so many centuries ago, saying: "You obviously know more about our history than we do". But when Roger went on to explain why it was so important to preserve these ancient sites, the Mayor merely laughed, telling him not to get worked up about a bit of old stonework that was of no use to anyone. Fortunately, since those days the Spanish have a much more enlightened attitude towards their inheritance.

As time went on, many ruined cottages were renovated and, before long, most had shaded terraces with smart walled gardens and swimming pools. On weekdays, the owners would tend their crops for an hour or two after doing their proper jobs in the towns and villages, then at weekends the whole family would arrive to pitch in and generally enjoy the country life.

Planning permission was not required to construct an agricultural store so long as it was no bigger than 50m^2 and these small square buildings began to be a familiar site in the *campo*. Before long, chimneys began to sprout from many of these "stores" and huge verandas with tiled roofs appeared along their fronts. Walls were then added around the terraces, creating rooms that almost doubled the size of the buildings. The final touch was to add a parapet around the flat roof of the original buildings - usually decorated with fancy bobbles - providing sunny roof terraces. Thus, the agricultural stores were stealthily transformed into very pleasant houses.

Money was flooding in from the EU. New motorways were being built everywhere and there was even a new road to Los Tablones, making the riverbed route to Motril redundant. Within a remarkably short period, the normal mode of transport in the countryside - motor scooters and battered old vans - was replaced by smart new cars and expensive 4x4 people carriers. It was no longer unusual to see women driving, and parking in Motril became increasingly difficult.

The transformation taking place in the countryside was entirely due to the availability of water. To qualify for a water supply and become a member of the *comunidad de regantes* (Community of Irrigators), it was necessary to demonstrate that you owned a proper *deposito* and sufficient land to require crop irrigation. The water was not properly treated like town water and not suitable for domestic use. Nevertheless, everybody had it piped into their houses for washing purposes. It was also against the rules to fill swimming pools with *Regantes* water, but one began to see *depositos* sunk into the ground near the *cortijos,* lined with blue tiles and surrounded by patios.

One of the big red water pipes had appeared about a hundred metres beyond our land. It came up the valley and ran along the far side of the track past a neighbouring *cortijo.* The occupants were an elderly couple who kept goats, grew some fruit and vegetables for the house and collected olives in the season.

Noticing that they had tapped into the source of water running past their house, we were keen to join in.

The office of the local *comunidad de regantes* was located on the outskirts of a small village on the way to Motril. It was nothing more than a hut beside the road where, in the evenings, groups of men would hang around - presumably discussing water. On this particular evening, the conversation came to an abrupt halt when two foreigners drew up in their little hire car. The men gazed in silence as we walked up to the building and tried the door. It was locked. They continued to watch in silence. Then Alison spied a small hand-written notice in the window which she deciphered as "Open Thursday 5.00 p.m. – 8.00 p.m.". Today being Wednesday, there was nothing for it but to try again tomorrow. Self-consciously, we walked back to the car, past the silent onlookers, and made our escape.

The following evening was more successful and we were able to introduce ourselves to the local *jefe* (boss) of the *comunidad de regantes*. Used to dealing with local farmers, he was surprised to see this clean cut English duo but he greeted us politely, indicating that we should be seated. He listened patiently to Alison's carefully prepared sentences explaining that we owned a *cortijo* near Los Tablones and wished to have water. He obviously understood our request, but the Spanish like to discuss things. Even when you buy a piece of meat in the market there will be a great deal of talk about how it will be cooked, whether the fat should be left on or not, what vegetables will go with it, how many people will be at the meal, whether or not it is a special occasion, etc. On the basis that everyone enjoys a good chat, our man began a long dissertation about water, pipes, pumps, mountains and *depositos*. At least, these were some of the words we could latch on to.

When he paused to ask some questions and we were completely stumped, he realised the futility of pursuing the conversation. Pointing at himself and carefully enouncing every word, he said:

"Mañana, iré a tu casa." (Tomorrow I will come to your house)

"Muchas gracias."

"A las once por la mañana."

This we understood and Alison replied in her best Spanish:

"Si, comprendo. Una reunión a las once. Hasta mañana." (Yes, I understand. A meeting at eleven o'clock. Until tomorrow).

Well, I was impressed. Alison's Spanish had now reached 'O' level GCSE; i.e extremely basic. She had recently given up the local Council's evening classes because her teacher had been informed that funding would only continue if <u>all</u> the pupils took the 'O' level exam. After leaving school, Alison had sworn never to take another exam; so, not wishing to upset the apple cart, she stopped attending.

Being local, the *jefe* knew how to find *La Caracola* and arrived on the dot. Asked to indicate the size of our plot, we paced the steps from the boundary behind the house to the carob tree in the front. He assumed that our land went all the way down to the river, which was correct, and began to make notes and calculations on his clipboard. Alison became concerned that he might assume that we had plans to bulldoze terraces down our hillside for growing crops. This would need a great deal of water for which we would have to pay. So she said:

No plantas. Agua para la casa solamente (No plants. Water for the house only).

This was definitely not the correct thing to say. He shook his head as though not comprehending and continued his calculations. Before Alison had a chance to repeat the sentence, I gave her a nudge and mouthed "No".

Underlining the final figure on the clipboard, our man explained his computations. Speaking slowly and in very basic Spanish for our benefit, we understood that because our land had restricted potential for cultivation, it would not require much water. We would therefore be charged the minimum rate. He gave us an enquiring look, saying:

"Bueno?"

I sensed from his raised eyebrows and amused expression that he had definitely understood Alison's remark.

"Bueno. Muchas gracias."

I had noticed that he had written down the word *"mahale"* with a total figure. This strange word also appeared in our *escritura de propiedad* (deeds), but we could find no translation in the dictionary. We asked Roger and he thought it was an old term for measuring how much land an ox could plough in one day. We agreed that it would have to be a tough old ox to plough anything on our bit of rocky hillside.

Thus, once we had revisited the office and received the paperwork, we became official members of the *comunidad de regantes* with the right to pump one hour of water per week from the big red pipe. But before an engineer from the *comunidad* could make the connection, we needed to build a little pump house next to the big pipe and run a hose to our *deposito*.

Pepe, our latest builder, was consulted. He understood exactly what was required and, of course, knew the *jefe* at the *comunidad*. He would be on the case as soon as his other work was finished. A price was agreed for the work including the pump, a long length of hose, and a *casita* (little house) for the pump. We paid him half the amount, shook hands, and saying that we would see him in September, left him to it.

Another short but successful trip - a splendid wardrobe in the bedroom, furniture and belongings shipped out from England, more walls painted and, most importantly, we could look forward to a permanent water supply.

Or could we?

CHAPTER SEVENTEEN
A Difficult Neighbour

Six weeks later, Roger, who now had a proper landline, telephoned with some ominous news. A distraught Pepe had begged him to let us know that all work on the water system had been stopped. The elderly man who lived in the house next to the big red pipe had refused to let him build the *casita,* claiming it was on his land. This, despite the fact that the *comunidad jefe* had told us exactly where to build it. There was nothing for it, but to rearrange our lives and make another flying visit.

Towards the end of May we arrived once again at *La Caracola* for a meeting arranged by Pepe with the *jefe* and the difficult elderly neighbour. Standing around the big red pipe, we were surprised to see a small crowd of interested parties and onlookers. News of the dispute had spread.

Pepe escorted us and the *jefe* to inspect the half-built casita. The Difficult Neighbour followed, waving his stick in the air and shouting angrily. There followed a heated exchange with the *jefe* pointing out to the man that when the big red pipe was installed, the *comunidad* had purchased three metres to each side. It was no longer his land. But the Difficult Neighbour continued to point at Pepe and shout abuse. Pepe, affronted at whatever was being said, added his voice to the affray. Then one of the bystanders, a man in his forties, stepped forward and somehow managed to calm things down.

Following a short discussion, the man left the group and headed in our direction. Frustrated at not being able to assist or understand what was going on, we had been witnessing the proceedings from a safe distance. Using simple words and gestures, the man explained that he was the son of our Difficult Neighbour, making it plain from his long-suffering expression that he found the old man's attitude equally unacceptable. He then proceeded to summarise what had been established. The siting of our *casita* on land owned by the *comunidad* was now accepted. What was not accepted was the hose to our *cortijo* running across our neighbour's land; the land in question being about six metres of unused scrub leading to the road. To avoid this scrap of wasteland, instead of laying the hose along the track straight to our house, we would have to run it beside the big pipe on *Comunidad* land right down to the bottom of the *barranco*, then all the way along to the border of our land and up again to our *deposito.*

This would require at least six times the amount of pipe and possibly a more powerful pump. A ludicrous and expensive solution. Furthermore, we would not be allowed to walk from the road across his scrubby little bit of land to gain access to our *casita*. This was incredibly inconvenient, as in order to turn the pump on and off and fill it with petrol, we would have to drive about a mile towards Motril to where the pipe went under the road, and then trudge along beside the pipe for quite a hundred yards or so.

What could we do? Now that there was no dispute regarding the siting of the *casita*, the *jefe* had nothing more to contribute. Where we ran our hose was not his concern. Grudgingly, we accepted the conditions and the man escorted us to his father, still engaged in animated discussion with Pepe, to announce that everything was agreed and the problem was solved. I shook the small gnarled hand of the old bastard, thanking him and saying *"amigos"* through gritted teeth. He did not shake hands with Alison, of course, because she was a woman.

The show now being over, everybody went home.

We stayed on for a few more days during which time Pepe built the *casita* and installed the petrol-driven pump, stomping to and fro across the taboo land as he did so. Moreover, he did not run the hose to our *deposito* all the way down the valley and up again to avoid the neighbour's land as discussed. He ran it just 20 metres or so down the big pipe then straight across the hillside.

Concerned at the inevitable repercussions, we reminded him of the agreement, but his terse reply indicated that nobody in their right mind would scramble to the bottom of the *branca* and up again carrying hundreds of metres of heavy hose pipe for no sensible reason. On several occasions we saw The Difficult Neighbour peering down at the work, but nothing was ever said. The thought processes of these Spanish country folk are sometimes unfathomable.

Water was only pumped through the red pipe on one day a week for a few hours, so all the farmers connected along this line had to remember when to turn on their pumps and fill their *depositos*. When the first available day came, Pepe set off to test the system while we waited expectantly at our *deposito*. A long pause. Nothing happened. Surely he must be there by now. How long would it take for water to travel that distance? Perhaps he cannot start the pump. Perhaps The Difficult Neighbour has cut the hose. Then there came a slight hiss of air. Did you hear that? The hiss grew louder and soon turned into a gurgle. Small spurts of water began to be coughed out. The spurts grew larger until, suddenly, glorious water was pouring into our *deposito*.

After about forty-five minutes the tank was nearly full and Pepe went to turn off the pump. Once again, he marched straight down the road and across the forbidden land. On future occasions when water was required, being cowards, we always went the long way round - just to be on the safe side.

Our joy at the thought of no longer having to conserve expensive water delivered by lorry was short lived. The little pump in the *deposito* that had happily operated for the past five and a half years suddenly gave up the ghost. We had all the water you could wish for in the *deposito* but nothing coming through the taps. A plumber was located, but by the time he had declared the pump beyond repair, ordered a new one and returned to install it, four days had passed. Meanwhile, in order for me to continue tiling and Alison to finish painting the outside of the house, water had to be carried in buckets.

As this unscheduled seven days in Los Tablones came to a close, we realised that the work on our little *cortijo* was nearing completion. All it needed now were final coats of paint in the living room and bedroom, give the place a general tidy up and we could actually move in!

It would make it an unprecedented three visits in one year, but we simply <u>had</u> to return in November.

Door to bathroom with gas heater cupboard on the right

Door to alcove above bath

With Pepe at the pump house

Roger's blue swimming pool tiles

La Caracola painted white

CHAPTER EIGHTEEN
We Move In At Last

Although Alison was keen to move in right away, I did not want to spend our first night in *La Caracola* with walls unpainted and the place littered with ladders, buckets and paint tins. I managed to persuade her that we should take advantage of our friends' generosity one more time and enjoy the comforts of *El Cortijuelo*.

Upon arrival at Malaga airport, the skies were untypically overcast and during the drive to Los Tablones we were suddenly engulfed in the most spectacular rainstorm. Traffic slowed to a crawl and when we eventually arrived at the turning to Los Tablones, the little road was slippery with water and mud washed down from the hillsides. Worse was to come, for when we arrived at *El Cortijuelo* the torrent had gouged out a deep gulley along one side of the short track leading to the house. There was nothing for it but to brave the torrential rain and collect a sufficient quantity of large stones from the surrounding area to fill the gulley so that the car could get across.

Ten minutes later, completely soaked, we arrived at the house and headed straight for the shower and some dry clothes. Once warm and dry and sitting in the kitchen cradling mugs of hot tea, the picture of the two of us scrabbling around in the mud and rain, picking up bits of rock seemed quite hilarious. It was all part of the adventure.

By the following morning the rain had ceased and the sun was shining once more. However, more rain damage awaited us at *La Caracola*. A stream of water was running through the living room into the kitchen and down the steps into the bathroom where it disappeared into the waste Eddie had installed in the floor in front of the shower. The source of the problem was a dip in the ground at the back of the house beside the bread oven where a lake had formed. As the walls of the house were made of mud and stones, water had seeped through. To prevent this happening again, Pepe filled the area with concrete.

It took us less than a week to finish painting the living room and bedroom and complete some more tiling. We then had a massive tidy up before the enjoyable task of unpacking the bed linen and kitchen equipment and arranging the furniture sent out from England. The old chest and bedhead that belonged to the house had previously been cleaned up.

After eight long years, we finally moved in to our little *cortijo* on Tuesday 12 November 1996. Against all odds, we had done it.

The remainder of the holiday was occupied with odd bit of tiling and paintwork but we mainly concentrated on finding items for the house in charity shops and street markets. An original black cooking pot for the *chiminea* and a remarkably cheap chandelier for the kitchen were purchased from the weekly flea-market in Nerja. Two round-bottomed water jugs for our recess feature were bought more expensively at an antiques shop where, on a subsequent trip we acquired a *lebrillo*. This essential item for any *cortijo* is a large bowl used mainly for mixing bread. It looked splendid perched on the low shelf to the right of the *chiminea*.

Six months later in May the following year, we experienced the first of many blissful holidays spent entirely in *La Caracola*. There were still jobs to be done in and around the house, but the pressure was off. There was time to sit and sun ourselves in our favourite place that afforded a wonderful view across the valley to the mountains. This was in the remains of an outbuilding opposite the bathroom that had a solid concrete floor and walls on two sides

providing shade during the afternoons. The only drawback being the difficulty of scrambling down the slope to get there, especially when carrying trays of food or drinks. Pepe was to carry out a few more jobs for us, so we asked him to include the construction of a flight of steps. These, we explained, were to be quaint and rustic, in keeping with an old *cortijo*. If they were irregular, so much the better.

He had previously agreed to extend Eddie's concrete pad in front of the house. As the ground dropped away in two directions, there was an opportunity to create interesting levels where we could place terracotta pots and planters for cacti and small trees. I drew a plan and to make sure that he understood, I indicated the terraces by scoring curved lines in the dirt with a stick. He kept repeating *"Si, si, si"* impatiently, indicating that further explanation was unnecessary.

The work was carried out during the months we were in England and upon our return we were aghast at the result. He had built up the lower sides of the slope with masses of rocks and laid a flat concrete pad in front of the house big enough to land a helicopter. The steps, far from being quaint and rustic, were four feet (120 cm) wide and formed with absolute precision.

When he turned up at the house, all smiles and eager to hear what we thought of his efforts, we hardly knew how to react. Proudly indicating the expanse of concrete, he began to talk about it at length. Seemingly there had been major problems that, with great difficulty and ingenuity, he had managed to overcome. The result, he felt, was a triumph.

There followed an embarrassing pause. We had no idea what to say or, indeed, how to say it. Not receiving the outpouring of thanks expected, Pepe assumed that we had not understood and repeated the whole speech, this time with a great deal of mime involving sweat pouring from his brow, aching arm muscles and terrible back pain, summing up with:

"Lo he construido muy plana. Terrazas no es necesario. Mucho mucho hormigón. Mucho hierro. Muy muy fuerte. mucho trabajo." (I build it very flat. Terraces not necessary. Masses of concrete. Much iron. Very very strong. Much work.).

Unlike Eddie's pad of concrete, it started to crack the following summer.

Assuming that his labours were now properly understood and appreciated - we had been forcing smiles and nodding - he moved on to point out the craftsmanship in the perfectly formed steps, demonstrating their magnificence by stomping up and down several times, puffing and blowing and growing puce with the exertion.

So delighted was he with his endeavours that we could not bear to see him deflated by hearing the truth. What was the point of hurting his feelings? Everything was solidly built and it would take dynamite to remove it now. So, being British, we smiled and offered our congratulations. The sting in the tail came when presented with the bill. It was far more than we had agreed. This was because of the *mucho mucho hormigón*, the *mucho hierro* plus the extra work in moving all those rocks and making the steps wider and more perfect. Obviously.

Although not to the same extent, there had been similar discrepancies between his estimates and final invoices in the past. So, sadly, although we enjoyed having Pepe around, we would not be using his services in the future. Besides, as Alison pointed out, he was not as decorative to have about the place as Robert or Fernando - or even Eddie.

Being without a builder put us in a bit of a quandary when, whilst spending an unprecedented three weeks in La Caracola the following year, we began to plan the next big project. We had the idea of constructing a second bedroom on top of the *deposito* so that the original little bedroom could be used as a dining room or occasional second bedroom.

The *deposito* sat in an L-shape of the building formed by the back of the kitchen and the side of the bedroom. One end was built against the wall of the kitchen but there was a gap of five feet or so (1.5m) between one side of the deposito and the bedroom. This was large enough to create a corridor from the kitchen with steps up to what would be the bedroom. My plan for the corridor incorporated a tall fitted cupboard on one side and a worktop with freezer below on the other. The area available for building measured around 18' x 13" (5.5m x 4m), a good-sized room. Conveniently, the flat roof of the storeroom Eddie had built down the slope against the side of the deposito could become the base for a balcony with views over the *barranco* to the Sierra Nevada.

The more time we spent in our little house, the less traumatic appeared the problems encountered during the renovation. True, there had been a few unlucky incidents along the way, but it had not been too awful, had it? Anyhow, we felt ready for another project. And with all that experience under our belts, surely the building of a simple extension should be pretty straightforward. Of course, this assumed that we could find yet another builder.

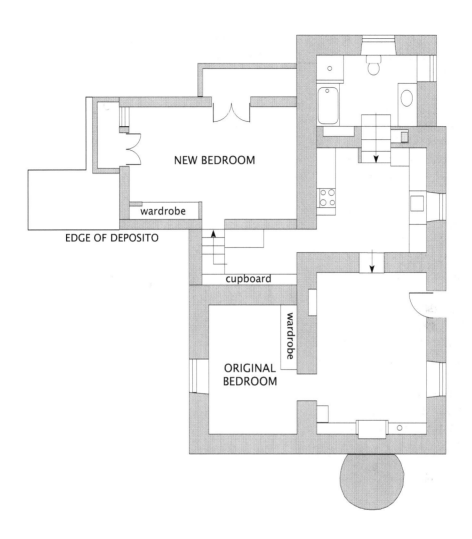

NEW BEDROOM

wardrobe

EDGE OF DEPOSITO

cupboard

wardrobe

ORIGINAL
BEDROOM

CHAPTER NINETEEN
Mike

Work at home was going well and there was some cash in the bank at last, but Alison had been through an emotional upheaval with the death of her father, followed eighteen months later by the loss of her mother. Harrowing months were spent with her two brothers arranging funerals, sorting out probate, and selling up the family home. Not a good time.

Our plans for building an extension to *La Caracola* had obviously been put on hold, but there came a time when our attention returned once more to the eternal problem in Spain - how to find a builder.

When discussing this over the telephone with Tony in Paris, he mentioned an Englishman whom he had met by chance one day while walking in the hills. Recently retired, the man had moved out from England and, with his son Mike, had built a house. Mike lived a few miles the other side of Motril and made a living from small building and decorating projects, mainly for British people. Tony suggested that it might be worth paying the gentleman a call.

There are very few dwellings in Los Tablones, so furnished with the name of the house and rough directions, the Englishman was not too difficult to locate. A charming man in his late sixties, he readily invited us in, always glad to see anyone who spoke English. Over coffee, he launched into a diatribe about the difficulty of building a house in Spain. He had encountered impenetrable bureaucracy when trying to buy the plot, and obtaining planning permission had been a nightmare. Fortunately, his son spoke Spanish but even he had enormous difficulty getting the water and electricity laid on. It had, he said, taken them a whole year to sort everything out.

We were not impressed.

The subject of our extra bedroom was touched upon and although his son did not normally work this far from his base, he offered to give him a call to see if he was interested. After a brief telephone conversation, it was arranged that Mike would meet us at *La Caracola* the following evening.

Mike and his wife had been living in Spain for more than two years. Their eleven-year old son attended a school in the seaside town of Salobreña where they lived. Being completely bi-lingual, he often made fun of his father's

106

pigeon Spanish. Mike's distinct northern accent, even when speaking Spanish, probably did not help.

Trained as an electrician, he worked in this trade for his first few months in the country. As his business grew, several of his clients wanted building work done but did not know where to go. They asked for his assistance and before long he had assembled a small team of Spanish builders who, we hoped, would shortly be let loose on our project.

Shown our plans, Mike was refreshingly positive and offered to prepare a detailed estimate. Having no means of communication at *La Caracola*, we met him a few days later in the bar of a hotel just outside Salobreña.

The price, once again substantially less than for similar work in the UK, was agreed and Mike became our fifth builder. He had several jobs to complete during the next six months, but could then be on site. This coincided conveniently with our next visit to Spain. He was going to supply all the materials and handle the whole job. It was all too simple. On the other hand, having been used to getting our hands dirty, we were feeling a bit left out. The quotation, as requested, did not include any decoration so at least we had that to look forward to.

At the beginning of November 1998, Mike with his assistant, Alfonso, and two brickies started mixing cement. The walls of our new bedroom rose at an amazing pace. Within days the roof beams were on, above which were laid thin planks of timber. The idea was to have a wooden ceiling supported by beams all stained a rich dark colour. This was a style we had seen in the mansions of Spanish nobility and we felt it would be very suitable for our smart new bedroom.

Building new bedroom on the *deposito*

The planks of timber needed to be treated with a preservative and stained before being installed, so we volunteered for that job. It was also essential to apply a liberal amount of "Carcomin" to every piece of timber in the house. This was a treatment against woodworm and, more importantly, the wood wasp that laid its eggs on the timber and when the larvae hatched, their chomping created serious holes. This was why Eddie had to replace the beam in the living room where one end had been entirely eaten away. The first realisation of how serious a problem this could be had occurred when we were staying at *El Cortiuelo*. Sitting quietly reading books one evening, we became aware of a kind of rustling sound, the source of which seemed to be emanating from a modern softwood chair used by Tony at his writing desk. On closer inspection, tiny grains of sawdust could be seen dribbling from several holes in the legs of the chair. The whole thing was alive with feasting creatures.

From then on, Alison became fanatical about every item of timber in *La Caracola*. Nothing constructed of wood was permitted to enter the house before it had been doused with Carcomin. She even had a little squirter to poke into any cracks or holes in case any little munchers might be lurking.

The floor tiles *(baldosas)* in the new bedroom were a modern version of the traditional clay *lozas* because, although less pleasing to look at, their polished finish was much easier to keep clean. Soon the roof was tiled, a window installed and glazed doors leading to small balconies on two sides. Mike had, of course, handled all the electrical work. It just remained to install a fitted wardrobe, plus the work surface and cupboard in the corridor from the kitchen. This he promised to complete before we returned a few months later.

During the building process, Mike remarked that our sitting place in the ruined outhouse was often untenable during the heat of the day and suggested that adding a simple roof would not be difficult or expensive. Good idea. So this was added to the list.

We left Spain incredibly pleased with ourselves. The new addition to *La Caracola* was built on time and looking better than we could have hoped. It was such a relief to know that since losing Eddie, we had finally found someone to whom we could communicate in English and trust to do an excellent job. Even better, the fact that Mike lived nearby and could interact with the locals meant that he was capable of solving any problems that might arise.

At least, that is what we thought until the phone rang in our houseboat one evening a few weeks before our next visit. It was Mike sounding somewhat aggrieved. That morning, he and Alfonso had travelled up to *La Caracola* with the cement mixer and all their gear to start work on the outhouse, to find that the neighbour in the house opposite had placed a chain across the track, fixed to posts cemented into the ground, barring access to his and our properties unless you had a key to the padlock. As they lived in town and were only there at weekends and some evenings, he was unable to talk to them. What was he to do?

From where we were, sitting in our houseboat on the river Thames, there was little we could suggest. Possibly, when we arrived in Spain we could get our *abogado* on to it. We understood that this was a public road and surely one had a right of access to one's property? Meanwhile, Mike was unable to proceed with the work as planned.

The following day, I telephoned Tony in Paris to have a moan about our latest crisis. He was sympathetic, but could not help seeing the funny side. The idea of some old Spanish peasant farmer going to all the trouble of erecting posts in concrete in order to close off a seldom used dirt track was ludicrous, but so typical of the sort of thing that happened in this part of the world.

Tony passed on the news of our predicament to Roger who phoned, saying that he had made contact with "The Old Bugger" (as he was to become known from then on) who had deliberately barred access to our property on the grounds that, at some time in the past, he had spent money maintaining the track. Therefore, he reasoned, if we wanted to use what he thought of as his track, then we should make a contribution. He was willing to give us a key to the padlock in return for a payment of 70,000 pesetas (a little more than £300). Roger said that this was outrageous and pure blackmail and we should fight it; but if we wanted him to hand over the money so that we could get on with our lives, that would be our decision. There was really no decision to make. Roger kindly sorted it out and we arranged for Mike to pick up the key.

*

It was around this time that I had an unexpected encounter in Hastings. On one of my regular visits to the Smugglers Adventure attraction, I happened to go into a local pub for a sandwich lunch. There, standing at the bar was Eddie. He greeted me with the familiar broad grin. Although a shadow of his former self, pale and extremely gaunt, it was really great to see that he was making a recovery.

On the counter before him was an unlikely glass of orange juice for which he apologised as if it were some kind of dishonour, explaining that he was under strict instructions to avoid the booze. He had been lucky to pull through from a serious collapse in Holland and had been warned that his liver could no longer take alcohol. This rare visit to Hastings was to get reacquainted with one of the female staff who worked in the caves. It had not worked out, he confided with a grin, because now that he was on the wagon she found him too boring.

Currently living in Oxfordshire, he was making ends meet by doing odd jobs such as installing kitchen cabinets; anything that did not involve hauling heavy bags of cement around. He enquired after Spain and I told him of the events leading up to our final move into *La Caracola*, stressing that his contribution had been crucial and his presence had been sorely missed during the final stages.

I mentioned that we always referred to the archway into the kitchen as "Eddie's arch". At this, he raised his eyebrows and said incredulously "Is that right?". Seemingly moved by this piece of information, he shook his head, saying quietly to himself "Eddie's arch". He turned away to take a sip of his orange juice and I swear that his eyes began to glisten. This unexpected reaction coupled with a memory of the Eddie of old who could carry four concrete blocks from the lorry when I could hardly manage two, brought a lump to my throat. Speech was beginning to be difficult so, before the whole thing became too emotional, I made my excuses and with a warm handshake took my departure. I turned at the door and my last image of Eddie was sitting on a bar stool, glass of orange juice raised in salute, a wistful smile on his whiskery face.

CHAPTER TWENTY
Bulldozers and Plastic

May 1999 and our arrival in Spain was tinged with excitement to see what Mike had built for us. Everything was even better than expected. The bedroom was spacious and once decorated it would become a most elegant addition to the house. The cupboards in the bedroom and corridor trebled our storage space and as soon as we could purchase a freezer to go under the new work surface, we could stock up with food rather than going to town every day. But the big surprise was the transformation of the outhouse. Sitting on the two existing stone walls and supported by a new pillar in the fourth corner was a solid concrete roof. Mike had also constructed a small stone parapet at the front – thoughtfully placed at a suitable height for your coffee cup or wine glass - and had laid the floor with tiles left over from the bedroom.

Now shaded from the sun, this idyllic nook – almost another room - was where we regularly ate our meals and where we first noticed small brightly coloured birds gliding past on the air currents and swooping down into the valley. We looked up these enchanting creatures and discovered that they were called bee-eaters and they usually nest in burrows tunneled into vertical earth or sand banks near riverbeds.

Mike had left the key for the wretched chain across our track with Roger. When we collected it, and reimbursed him for the blood money, he mentioned a brand new hose he had seen running from The Old Bugger's house, down the hillside and along to the big red pipe. The cost of this would have been in the region of 70,000 pesetas (a little more than £300). Funny, that. We continued with the nonsensical inconvenience of locking and unlocking the chain for a while until one day, surprise surprise, it disappeared. Never to be seen again.

More annoying for us was the new wire fence he had erected along the track opposite our house. Now that he had plenty of water, the land at the back of his *cortijo* had been bulldozed with the rocks, boulders and vegetation scraped to one side, creating a flat surface for lorry loads of topsoil. Where we used to wander on this open land amongst the olive trees was now a fenced off field.

In the house, we had a couple of unpleasant experiences: the first was when we arrived and I went to use the lavatory. Upon lifting the lid, I discovered the entire bowl to be smeared with dried excrement. That was before I noticed that some creature had been chewing away at the wooden seat from the inside. There was a jagged crescent-shaped chunk missing from the front of the seat about five inches (12cm) wide and two inches (5cm) deep. Presumably, a rat had found its way into the overflow pipe of the pooh hut and, there being no water in the system, had scampered up the soil pipe. Thank goodness we had left the lid down.

The second incident also occurred in the lavatory when, in the middle of one night, Alison was answering the call of nature. Sitting there, half asleep, she was jolted into alarmed wakefulness at the sight of an enormous bright red centipede scuttling across the floor towards her. Remembering that this was the very insect Roger had warned her and her mother was much more dangerous that a scorpion, she cautiously rose to her feet, took a deep breath, then leapt over the monster to land beside the door. With what I consider bravery way beyond the call of duty, rather than wake me to assist, she took a plastic salad bowl from the kitchen, returned to the danger zone, and plonked it over the creature. To her horror, the centipede carried on walking, pushing the plastic bowl across the floor. It was that strong. Hurrying back to the kitchen, she grabbed a heavy saucepan and gingerly placed it on top of the bowl. That stopped it.

In the morning, when I lifted the saucepan, the salad bowl immediately began its travels. Armed with broom, shovel and bucket, the big red creepy crawly was finally trapped and removed from the premises. Remarkably few insects were ever found in the house and we decided that it must have entered during the building process when the walls and windows were not properly sealed.

Putting aside these minor irritations, the remainder of our stay consisted of eating, drinking, snoozing (which had always been the aim of this enterprise) with a few hours a day decorating the new extension. We even managed to get in some sightseeing, including an exploration of some of the picturesque villages high up in the Alpujarra mountains.

Some of these villages had become haunts for hippies seeking a simple life during the 1970s and 1980s. Dreadlocks, nose rings and floating clothing were still very much in evidence, although some of the faces showed the passage of time. The cuisine in theses villages is specific to the area and over the years we have made many trips to sample the excellent food. Pampaneira became a favourite village where there are a series of shops with wonderful arrays of locally manufactured carpets and hangings at incredibly cheap prices. On one occasion, it was a hot sunny day in October, we left the coast and after

Carpet in Pampaneira

travelling for a little more than an hour, were surprised to arrive at a village that was covered in snow with everyone wearing boots, scarves and heavy rainwear. Aware that we were heading into the mountains, we had brought light woolen jumpers, but these were totally insufficient for these freezing conditions.

Towards the end of our holiday, we experienced an alarming event. One night, whilst sleeping snugly in our original bedroom, I was roused by a fearsome roaring sound and the rattling of the front door. Half awake, I imagined some angry giant trying to break in. Then, the lamps on the bedside tables began to shake and rattle. Alison sat up and muttered: "Earthquake". We could feel the bed vibrating... and then it all stopped. We lay there in anticipation of more tremors, but all was still. When we next spoke to Mike, he confirmed that there had been an earthquake in our area. Living some miles away, it had been less dramatic for him, but he did get out of bed because of the noise, worried that his son had got up in the night and fallen down the stairs. Apart from that unexpected incident, everything was perfect. Our dream house was complete.

Sitting out Place before painting plus Pepe's steps

Old bedroom now a dining room

NEW BEDROOM

CHAPTER TWENTY-ONE
Up For Sale

During the following two years, whenever life became stressful in England, there was always the thought of that little *cortijo* waiting for us in the sunshine. However, there was a 'but'. And the 'but' was looming larger with every month that passed.

The gradual erosion of the distant view by the appearance of more and more *invernaderas* on the other side of the *barranco* was distressing. The tops of beautiful hills had been sliced off to make flat areas for these vast plastic greenhouses and now they were beginning to encroach nearer home. The Difficult Neighbour had erected an *invernadera* and it was only time before our nearest neighbour, The Old Bugger, decided to follow suit. Growing crops like cabbages, onions and potatoes, entailed many back-breaking weekends with his entire family – sons, daughters, spouses – labouring in the hot sun planting and harvesting everything by hand. One could appreciate the appeal of a large greenhouse where tomatoes and fruit could be grown more easily and more profitably. However, an *inverdera* on his land would be just the other side of the track, a stone's throw from our front door. The Old Bugger, being quite ancient, was seen less often these days and his son, a member of the *Guardia Civil*, was taking over. The younger generation was not so keen on toiling in the fields, so there was good reason to believe that a plastic monstrosity on our doorstep was likely. We had also been told that, at certain times of year, they could be quite smelly. Not a happy prospect.

Reluctantly, very reluctantly, we concluded that it was time to make a move. If *La Caracola* could be sold, perhaps we could find a plot of land somewhere nearer Malaga. The intention was to spend more time in Spain. I was nearing retirement and Alison could adjust her bookings to create more free time.

By then, Roger had sold his property in Los Tablones and he and Pepe were living a few miles from the small town of Velez Malaga, less than forty-five minutes from Malaga airport. They had bought a house that was being completely renovated, with Roger's flair for design in evidence everywhere. The garden now boasted a large swimming pool and they had planted a variety of exotic trees and cacti to supplement what was growing there already.

According to Roger, one of the great appeals of the area was that the neighbours were all delightful. "Not like Los Tablones", he said "where they are all mad!" Delightful neighbours? That, we thought, would make a pleasant change. Moreover, *invernaderas* were not allowed in the province of Malaga. No plastic!

But wait a bit! Building another house in Spain? Surely we were not planning to put ourselves through all that stress and heartache again?

On the other hand...

This time it would be totally different. We knew the pitfalls, we had a better grasp of the language, Mike was more than willing to undertake a building project, and we had the comfort of our friendly *abogado* to ensure that everything was tied up legally from the start. What could go wrong?

All fired up, we made an appointment to see Juan Alvarez, but when informed of our intention to sell *La Caracola,* his reaction came as a complete shock. He raised his eyebrows and, with a heavy sigh, stated:

"No es posible." (It is not possible).

I turned to Alison. *"No es posible!"* What does he mean *"no es posible?"* Is he saying we cannot sell our own house?"

Ignoring the interruption, he continued. Did we not realise that, although we had the *escritura*, we did not have the *primera ocupación*. We had never heard of this and had no idea what it was. The *primera ocupación*, he explained - as everyone knows - is the document you must have before you move into a house (a small detail not previously mentioned). Moreover, without the *primera ocupación* it is illegal to do electrical work, install gas bottles or, indeed, carry out any form of renovation or construction.

Alison, who was able to follow this much closer than I, asked why we had not been given this document if it was so vital. He shrugged, saying dismissively: "Los Tablones".

Apparently, a *cortijo* near Los Tablones, the back of beyond, was of little interest to the *ayuntamiento*. So it was not important. However, in order to sell, one had to have all the correct documentation. He would have to visit *La Caracola* with an architect, make plans of the extension and apply for retrospective planning permission for all the work carried out. Only then could he obtain the *primera ocupación.*

How long would all this take? Juan Alvarez estimated a few weeks. From bitter experience, we knew that a few weeks dealing with Spanish bureaucracy could end up as a few years. Nevertheless, he assured us this was totally possible and, five months later, when we turned up at his office on our next trip to Spain, he handed over the document.

In October 2000, La Caracola was placed on the market with two agents in Motril who gave similar valuations and a sale price was agreed at the equivalent of £30,000. We had estimated that we had, over the years, spent a total of £24,000 on the property, so we were happy with that. As with all agents, they were confident of a quick sale so, having tidied up and made the house as presentable as possible, we waited for the flood of eager viewers.

A week went by and nothing happened. During the second week, one of the agents found two possible buyers. The other agent never managed to drum up any interest at all. Both viewings consisted of groups of men who spent most of the time discussing the land. What we thought would be the main selling point, the interior design and layout of our beautiful home, only warranted a peremptory glance. It became obvious that the Spanish had no interest in country cottages and fine views. Mountains they saw every day of their lives. Their sole concern was the potential for growing crops. There was a certain amount of flattish ground in front of the *cortijo*, but the major part of our land stretching down to the *barranco* was pretty steep. We had witnessed bulldozers working at crazy angles carving out great chunks of hillsides to create terraces for *invernaderas,* but our precipitous slope was probably not worth the effort.

During the second of the viewings, there was a strange occurrence when the Difficult Neighbour, presumably having got wind of our intention to sell, put in an appearance carrying a bucket of white paint and a large brush. While the agent was talking to the prospective buyers in front of the house, the old man started shouting, working himself up into a complete frenzy. He then began to daub a white line across the road. This was presumably to make the point that the road from that point on belonged to him - which it certainly did not. Meanwhile, the men continued their conversation, nobody taking the slightest notice of this extraordinary charade. We, on the other hand, were concerned that the old fool's behavior was not exactly assisting the prospects of a sale. So we approached him, all smiles and friendliness.

Gracias. Esto es muy útil. Muy bueno. Muchas gracias. (Thank you. This is very helpful. Very good. Many thanks.)

119

Having prepared himself for a really good argument, the polite British approach completely took the wind out of his sails. He had no idea how to react so, muttering darkly, he brandished his brush at the group of visitors, who happened to be looking the other way, and took himself off.

Despite this disappointing lack of interest in *La Caracola*, it was early days and we determined to continue the search for our next Spanish home. Roger introduced us to a farmer who was planning to sell building plots on a section of his land near Velez Malaga, but it was a long term project and the location was not appealing. Various agents showed us a number of plots of land and *cortijos* in need of restoration along the Costa del Sol, the coastline of the province of Malaga, but for one reason or another they were all unsuitable. The only properties that did catch our eye were way beyond our price bracket.

It was suggested to us that the best way to find a reasonably priced piece of land in the hills was to choose an area, visit the bars and chat up the locals. We were not in the habit of frequenting bars and our ability to chat up locals was extremely limited. However, it was all part of the Quest and probably worth a go. We settled upon an area that was a good forty minutes nearer to Malaga than Los Tablones where, we were assured, *invernaderas* were not allowed. It was near a charming seaside town called Almuñécar (pronounced "Al-moo-nyeka").

Turning our backs to the sea, we headed up into the hills. The first stop was at a remote cluster of houses with a small village shop. There was also a bar that did not look too threatening, so we entered and ordered coffee. The only other customers, three locals drinking beer at a table in the corner, acknowledged us briefly before resuming their conversation.

Seated on stools at the bar counter with our coffees, Alison asked the landlord if he knew of any land or ruined houses for sale in the area. He thought for a moment and then raised his voice to address the locals. An animated discussion ensued with everyone joining in. As far as we could tell from the pointing and gestures of two of the men, there was definitely something up the road. The name "Rubio" was repeated several times. Was this a person or a place?

When the babble died down, the barman explained that there was an old house in need of restoration some two or three kilometres from the village. We had to speak to a man called Rubio in Almuñécar. He lived in an area called La Moruña, but nobody knew the house number or even the street. Just ask for Rubio. Everybody knows Rubio.

Andalucia does not go in for proper street maps and that evening we were sorely in need of an A-Z. The tourist information office was closed, of course, but a man accosted in the street provided directions to La Moruña. It was a modern estate of small terraced houses on the outskirts of the town. Feeling a bit foolish, we wandered the streets enquiring of anyone we met: *"La casa de Rubio?"* It was not long before a group of young boys chatting on a street corner answered with a chorus of *"Si, si, si."* and escorted us excitedly to a house a few doors away. For them, it was probably the most interesting event of the week. One of the youths stepped forward to knock on the door, then joined the others to witness the proceedings.

A tall muscular man in his forties opened the door and regarded us suspiciously. *"Rubio?"* Alison enquired; although if we had known that *rubio* in Spanish simply meant blonde, the question might have been redundant. In contrast to the majority of his countrymen, Rubio sported an unruly shock of fair hair that seemed at odds with his dark weather-beaten complexion.

"Si" he said, looking even more puzzled. *"Que quieres?"* (What do you want?)

Alison began with her usual opener: *"Hablo un poco de español solamente. Lo siento."* (I speak a little Spanish only. Sorry). She always found this phrase useful for setting up the ground rules for any conversation. She then tried to convey with her few verbs – all in the present tense - the purpose of our visit. As soon as he grasped the meaning of the disjointed sentences concerning a village in the hills, a man in a bar, a *cortijo* for sale, and talk to Rubio, his bemused expression transformed into a look of amusement. We wanted to see his property? He would be delighted to show us his property. Would we care to meet him at the bar in the village this time tomorrow?

Thus, the following evening saw us climbing high into the hills until we came to a deserted building standing beside the single track road. To either side, the land dropped steeply away to valleys far below. To the north were the spectacular mountains of the Sierra Nevada while to the south there was an eagle's eye view of the coastline. Alison was particularly struck by the wonderful silence.

Facing the road at the far end of the house, the front door opened into a sizeable space one imagined would be the living room, were it not for the remains of cooking facilities lining the wall opposite. A forlorn-looking work surface with a large sink encrusted with spiders' webs was leaning at a crazy angle because some of the supports had given way. Above and along the wall, rusty old conduit tubes with wires poking out showed where the electrical plug sockets had once been. Smoke and grease stains on the wall signified that some serious cooking had taken place here. It all became clear when Rubio explained that this room used to be a bar, owned and run by his father.

Having cleared that up, we went on to look at the rest of the building. Apart from rotting doors and window frames, the house was in pretty good shape. Internal walls in all of the four rooms were sound and the floors were solid, although the tiles would need replacing. To make the place habitable, a good deal of work was required, but nothing that Mike could not handle.

It goes without saying that with the stunning views and the possibility of restoring the property without too much difficulty, we were feeling very positive. The excitement became more intense when we discovered that the price was well within our budget, always assuming that *La Caracola* was sold for something near the asking price. Our enthusiasm was only slightly dampened when Alison, enquiring how long the place had been unoccupied, thought that Rubio answered: "Not since the murder"!

Although not a word she had thought necessary to learn, *Asesinato* sounded very much like Assassination. But surely she had misunderstood. Alison responded with her usual: *"No comprendo."*

Patiently, using simple phrases, Rubio recounted how one night, years ago, there was an argument in the bar, and someone was shot. I could not entirely follow the Spanish so Alison translated for me. Rubio, mistaking our stunned expressions for a continuing lack of understanding, mimed firing a pistol while making an explosive noise with his mouth, then acted being hit in the chest and dying with eyes staring and mouth open. Alison confirmed:

"Hombre muerto!" (Man dead!)

"Si. Pistola. Muerto." (Yes. Pistol. Dead)

"Qui está muerto?" (Who is dead?)

"Mi padre" (My father)

"Su padre!" (Your father!)

Relieved that we finally understood, a broad smile spread across his face.

"Si, si, si. Mi padre."

Although he was grinning happily, it seemed appropriate to mumble sounds of commiseration before getting back to the business of the day. We told him that we liked the house but needed time to think about it. I was beginning to have slight reservations about the place as I was having visions of walking into the living room and coming face to face with a ghost. Alison told me to grow up.

Then came the news that effectively put the kibosh on the whole enterprise. When asked how much land came with the property, we were told *"No hay ninguna tierra."* (There is no land). When Alison explained that it was important for us to have a garden, he shrugged apologetically, saying, *"No es posible."*

A moment later, his face lit up and saying, *"otra posibilidad."* (another possibility), indicated that we should follow him further up the hill. At some distance from the building, he stopped and pointed at the land beside the road, explaining to Alison that he was willing to sell us a plot he owned here. We could, he said, build ourselves a brand new house. To show us the extent of the land, he walked us round the boundary. It was not very large, but there was plenty of room for a small garden and even a swimming pool. He said it was 600 square metres. Perfect.

Electricity could be laid on from the supply at the old bar. There was no water, but Rubio assured us that the local farmer would let us have a supply from a nearby *deposito*. With our experience of neighbouring farmers, we viewed this idea with a certain amount of skepticism. We would not go ahead unless our *abogado* could draw up an absolutely "water tight" agreement.

The price mentioned was less than we had previously been discussing, and the thought of building a house to our own design with these wonderful views was very exciting.

Not wishing to appear too keen, we said that we would consult our lawyer and talk to Rubio in two days time. This being amicably agreed, we all headed back to Almuñécar.

Once again, the meeting with our *abogado* did not go as expected. Firstly, Juan Alvarez was concerned about securing a satisfactory agreement with the local farmer for a permanent water supply and, secondly, he was not at all happy about buying a property via some person we knew nothing about.

Pointing an accusing finger, he reminded us of *La Caracola*, expressing amazement at our determination to buy houses from strangers in bars. This, he emphasized, was not a good idea.

Nonetheless, we begged him to pursue the project as the asking price for 600 metres of land in that location was just too good to miss. At the mention of 600 metres, his ears pricked up and, striving to assume a sorrowful expression, he informed us that, by law, we needed a minimum of 2,500 square meters to build a house in the *campo*. This was to stop houses being built willy-nilly all over the countryside. Juan Alvarez spread his hands in a gesture of regret, although he could not disguise his relief at discovering a legal reason to save us from our folly.

Disappointed and duly chastened, we thanked him for his advice and took our leave. All that remained was to get out the dictionary and compose some sentences to tell Rubio why we could not buy his house.

CHAPTER TWENTY-TWO
Antonio and Josefina

A few days later, when Mike enquired if we were having any success finding a building plot, we regaled him with the Rubio fiasco. The mention of Almuñécar reminded him of a development opportunity he had recently viewed and rejected. A building worker he had occasionally employed, now retired, wished to sell off half his land. It included a crudely built two-room house that was only used as a base when tending their fruit trees and other crops as they had a proper house in the town. Mike said that it was probably not suitable for us, being a bit remote and with difficult access along a dry riverbed. We told him that, on the contrary, this sounded just like our cup of tea and we would very much like to have a look.

The drive along the dry riverbed in Mike's 4x4 was longer than anticipated and pretty bumpy. After about a third of a mile, there was a turn-off into a rough track that soon became a tarmac road rising steeply, twisting and turning around the hills for another mile or so. Alison became concerned every time she thought the vehicle was travelling too close to the edge of a vertical drop, but my main worry was that we might meet someone coming the other way. Mike, who was entirely used to this kind of

Rio Seco - dry riverbed

terrain, said one always hoped to be on the inside against the rock face so that the other chap had to squeeze past beside the drop. Meeting a large lorry was no fun because they would not back up. A car or van would be expected to reverse down or up to the nearest wider section or, if you were lucky, into the gateway of some *finca* (country property).

Narrow roads with vertical drops

The road eventually flattened out and turned once more into a dirt track. Then, rounding a corner, we caught our first glimpse of what might become our new Spanish home. The building was perched on the side of a steep slope with olive trees interspersed with almonds and avocados on several terraces. It was squat and ugly, but there was an attractive paved area in front of the house surrounded by a series of high arches painted a pleasant soft yellow.

As soon as we pulled up at the entrance to the property the owners appeared, walking down from the terraces where they had been working. They greeted us warmly before opening the front door to their ramshackle little house.

In his mid sixties, Antonio had the healthy tan of a man who spent his life working in the open air. Unlike many of his compatriots, he was softly spoken and had an air or serenity about him. Josefina, his wife, a few years younger, was an attractive woman with an abundance of well-groomed fair hair above a kindly face. She bubbled over with enthusiasm and always took the lead in conversations, while Antonio regarded her with an amused expression, appearing to be genuinely interested in what she had to say. They were both about five foot tall (1m 53cm) which Alison found most excellent. Being five foot tall herself, as far as she was concerned this was the correct size for a person.

Inside the ramshackle house there were just two rooms. At the back was a bedroom with a stunning view to the east across an extremely wide valley rising to mountains on the other side. Roads and villages could be seen far below with the sea visible to the south. The other half of the house was a gloomy living room with some basic cooking facilities in one corner consisting of a small work surface with a couple of gas rings connected to a Calor gas bottle. There were no

Antonio and Josefina

washing facilities. The only running water was at a sink outside where the tap was connected to a hose running from their *deposito* further up the hill.

The entire house, no more that 23' x 23' (7m x 7m), was disappointingly small. Antonio, sensing our concern, beckoned us outside. Sandwiched between the house and some sort of outbuilding was a long flight of concrete steps leading down to a lower terrace. Constructed on a steep slope, the rear of the house was twice as tall as the front. At the bottom of the steps, a door led into a long thin storeroom created between the front wall of the building and the slope of the hill behind. The ceiling was quite low and while this was not a problem for Alison and the Spanish duo, I found it claustrophobic. Mike suggested that with the addition of some windows it could be turned into a useful room.

Emerging from the dark store, we were shown the two-story brick construction on the other side of the steps. The lower level had a wire mesh front and was home to a number of chickens.

We then climbed back up the steps to be shown the storage space above. Antonio opened the padlocked metal door and we could see that it contained various tools, boxes and sacks. Pointing to a wooden barrel perched on some concrete blocks in a corner, he informed us proudly that it contained wine made from his own grapes.

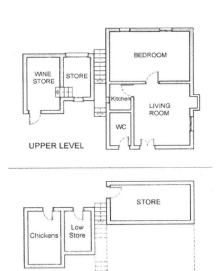

This was the extent of the property, but despite the limited amount of living space, presumably we could expand the main building during the process of renovation. There was concern about the lack of water and electricity, but Mike was confident that electricity could be organised. There were poles everywhere with cables running to the nearby houses. Water was not a problem as Antonio had a large *deposito* on his land and we were assured that a supply could be arranged as part of the deal.

We looked at each other and edged away from the others, pretending to look at the view. "It's perfect", said

Alison. "Absolutely", I agreed. Trying not to look too eager, we casually strolled back to the others and I said to Mike: "We want to buy it". Alison added: "Yes, but can we confirm the price before we say anything?"

Mike had been a bit vague about how much Antonio and Josefina had in mind, having said that he thought it was around £16,000. When consulted, Antonio stated a sum of 4,500,000 pesetas and there was a tense pause while this was translated into sterling. It did indeed amount to around £16,000. Later, we discovered that this figure was based upon how much they needed to buy a four-wheel-drive van and materials to build a small *cortijo* on their land above.

This was an amount we could find. The major cost of all the renovation work would have to wait until after the sale of *La Caracola*. But that was alright. Mike was given the nod and our delighted neighbours-to-be were informed that we had fallen in love with the place and, subject to a legal agreement, were happy to pay the asking price.

Smiling broadly, Antonio clasped my hand in his firm grip and shook it vigorously while Josefina gave Alison a hug and a kiss on both cheeks. Antonio said a few hurried words to Josefina and she disappeared into the house, returning with five drinking glasses. These were filled by Antonio with rosy red liquid from the wine barrel in the store and handed out. Glasses were raised. The transaction - and our friendship - were both cemented as we all cried "salud!" with Antonio adding his favourite toast:

"Dinero y amor." (Money and love)

The wine was powerful stuff, dry but reasonably drinkable if one persevered. Alison, who never takes alcohol, pretended to take a sip, feigning surprise and pleasure (well, she is an actress). Her glass was then surreptitiously emptied into mine as space became available. By the time I had consumed two glasses of Antonio's home brew in double quick time, the world and everyone in it appeared wonderful, if a little out of focus, and it was just as well that Mike would be driving us back down the mountain track.

It was arranged that Mike would contact Antonio the following day to exchange details of lawyers and with much waving, good wishes and thank-yous, we headed back to Almuñécar where we had left our car. On the way, Mike had to admit that the position of the house with the spectacular views was much better than he remembered. Perhaps, as a builder, he had been disappointed by the depressing little building and had failed to take in the splendid setting.

During the drive, Alison and I talked excitedly about various possibilities for renovation and extension, only to have our enthusiasm quashed when Mike interrupted with some professional advice.

"Hire a bulldozer. Knock the whole thing down. It's a totally crap building. You would be wasting your money trying to prop it up. Design something to suit your own needs. Build a proper house on the site."

Upon reflection, this did seem sound advice and, having successfully designed the interiors of two houseboats, I had always fancied the idea of designing a house from scratch. Mike promised that, as soon as we had officially acquired the plot and come up with a design acceptable to the planning authorities, within twelve months we would be moving in. To speed up the legal and planning processes, we came to an arrangement whereby he would keep an eye on the proceedings, charging for his time accordingly.

Allowing a few days for *abogado* to speak to *abogado*, we made an appointment to see Juan Alvarez. It was all good news. He had been in touch with Antonio's lawyer and everything was in order. This time, everything was to be done by the book.

Juan Alvarez then asked what purchase price we would like him to put on the official sale agreement, suggesting a sizeable cash payment to the vendor with a declaration of the remainder as the official price. This all sounded a bit dodgy and we queried the legality of what he was proposing. Rejecting our concerns with a dismissive wave of the hand, he explained that this was perfectly normal in Spain to avoid paying unnecessary tax. Antonio's *abogado*, who went by the unusual name of Antonio Enrique de Weert Waltravens, was happy with whatever figure we decided upon, so everything was fine.

It turned out that Weert Waltravens was a Dutch name, which might have given us pause for thought, only it was hardly fair to condemn an entire race because of one unfortunate incident in Los Tablones – or several unfortunate incidents if one counted our experiences in Rotterdam.

Upon our return to the UK, a 10% deposit of the "official price" was transferred to Mike's bank account, to be passed on to Juan Alvarez.

Six weeks later, in April 2001, Mike informed us that the two *abogados* had drawn up the sale agreement and were ready to receive a cheque for the remaining 90% of the "official price". A cheque made out to Antonio Paramo Martin was duly dispatched to our *abogado*.

Before setting off for Spain later that month, we collected the "unofficial sum" in cash from a Spanish bank in London. This was stuffed into our hand luggage, hoping that no questions would be asked at Customs.

Fortunately, we had sent more funds to our Spanish bank account because Juan Alvarez, after expressing himself happy with progress so far, presented an invoice for 17,000 pesetas (about £600) to cover his fees to date, plus a further bill of 13,000 pesetas (£460) for 6% tax and 0.5% stamp duty. And there was more to come.

A new Title Deed (the *escritura de propiedad*) legally stating who owned which portion of the segregated land had to be drawn up. This was a lengthy process with papers to sign when we were not going to be available, so we agreed to give Juan Alvarez Power of Attorney to buy and sell the properties on our behalf. While filling in the relevant form, he casually mentioned that his charge for this service was a surprisingly steep 15,000 pesetas (£540). When our signatures had been appended to the document, we were asked to take it to the *notario's* office to be signed and stamped. Here, the official who did the deed, taking all of five minutes, presented us with a further bill of 7,060 pesetas (£250).

All in all, a very expensive morning.

That evening found us wandering the streets of Almuñécar self-consciously clutching a small holdall bursting with wads of cash, the unofficial payment for the property. Antonio and Josefina lived high up in the old part of town within a maze of narrow cobbled alleyways. Their two-story terraced house was eventually located not far from Almuñécar's castle. Antonio opened the door and after muted greetings, the holdall was handed over and the money counted out on the dining room table. This took some time. That number of pesetas required a great deal of counting and Antonio went through the process twice. Very little was said. Even Jopsefina remained silent. This was men's work.

Finally satisfied, Antonio signed the receipt we had typed out, keeping a copy for himself, and the business was concluded. Politely declining an offer of refreshments, we shook hands and took our leave, heartily relieved that this whole clandestine affair was behind us. Furtively handing over wads of cash to foreign strangers in the dead of night was like something out of a 1950's B movie. However, the deed was done. There was no going back.

Rather worryingly, nothing had been heard from either of the estate agents regarding the sale of *La Caracola* and their failure to find any interest whatsoever was now a serious concern.

First view of house from the south

House from north with wine store in left foreground

Steps to lower terrace. Door to storeroom on left

Door to storeroom on lower terrace to become bedroom

CHAPTER TWENTY-THREE
Mister Cortijo

Strolling around Motril one morning to buy fresh bread and provisions for the day, we happened to stumble across an unusual looking estate agent. Located in a side street, it had large lettering above a very small shop front proclaiming "MISTER CORTIJO". The window itself contained not a single photo or details of any properties for sale or rent whatsoever. In fact, it was completely bare except for a sign (in English!) stating that they were experts in buying and selling properties 'on line'. This was terribly *avant garde* for Motril in 2001 and as we had lost faith in the two traditional agents, it seemed sensible to investigate.

Problem. The door was locked. A rather unhelpful note taped to the glass read: "If the shop is closed I am somewhere else". Mister Cortijo was either a jolly joker or not very bright. Intrigued to discover the truth, we returned the following day and had more luck. The shop was sparsely furnished with just a single filing cabinet and two desks. One was unoccupied but behind the other sat Mister Cortijo tapping away on a computer. The slim pasty-faced young man with neat black hair wearing a natty grey suit, looked eagerly up as we entered, pleased – possibly surprised - to have a customer. Greeting us in almost perfect English, he enquired whether we were interested in buying or selling. When informed of our situation, he explained that his business was exclusively conducted on-line and pretty well all of his clients were either English or Scandinavian. His fees were very reasonable and as he expressed total confidence in finding a buyer within weeks, we agreed to go ahead. That afternoon he arrived at *La Caracola* on his motorbike to take photographs. Largely ignoring what we thought were some of the best views and features in the house, he used his expensive-looking camera to take a quick snap in each room plus one of the exterior and declared himself satisfied. He then roared off down the track in a cloud of dust. This was a disappointing to say the least and we imagined that Mister Cortijo would fair no better than our other agents.

The following day we had to close up the house and head back to London. Almost immediately upon arrival, I fired up the computer and found Mister Cortijo's website – and there we were. The photos were fantastic and the description of the property was brief but spot on. Perhaps he did know what he was doing.

The surprising phone call came three days later. Mister Cortijo had two possible buyers, both English and both extremely keen. One was offering the asking price, site unseen. The other had arranged to fly out that weekend for a viewing. The woman eager to buy our *cortijo* was willing to pay the non-returnable deposit immediately in order to secure the deal. Mister Cortijo recommended that we should accept the offer so that the second person had time to cancel an unnecessary trip.

It was hardly a difficult decision. Mister Cortijo would sort out the paperwork and pass on a cheque for the 10% deposit to our *abogado* to whom we had given Power of Attorney to handle the sale. The completion would take a few weeks, at which point we would fly out to clear the house of our belongings. All this was happening in June 2001.

With the impending sale of *La Caracola*, serious thought could now be given to the design of the new house. Mike had arranged for the land to be measured, having checked with the planning office at the *ayuntmiento* that permission to build a new house in our area would be granted so long as there was a minimum of 2,500 square metres of land. The surveyor came up with a measurement of 2,588 square metres, so that was all right. We could build exactly what we wanted.

Hours were spent on the computer. So many decisions. Did we want a traditional style *cortijo* or a modern villa? Did we need more than two bedrooms? Should there be a kitchen/diner or a separate dining room? Would it be sensible to design terraces to incorporate a swimming pool at a later date?

A great deal of time was spent agonising over the layout of the kitchen to ensure that everything was in the right place. One of my obsessions is to ensure that the simple act of making a pot of tea does not involve a half-mile hike. The kettle has to be near the tap, and the teapot, mugs and cutlery drawer all have to be within reach, as have the shelf or cupboard for the sugar, tea and coffee. Similarly, the fridge for the milk should not be the other end of the kitchen. The same principle applies to pots, pans and cooking utensils being handy for the cooker. Alison is equally obsessive about having proper storage and drew up lists of every item she could think of that required a home. Armed with this, I incorporated the requisite number of cupboards, shelves and drawers.

Having worked out the ideal amount of space and the relationship between all the rooms, a floor plan began to emerge. Mike had advised us to build exactly what we wanted but when everything, including the kitchen sink, was on the plan, the building turned out to be somewhat larger than anticipated. The drawings were dispatched to Mike for comment and costing in the knowledge that adjustments might have to be made if it was all beyond our budget. Mike's initial comment upon receiving the plans was that the name "Southfork" sprang to mind. This being the oil millionaire's home in the then popular television series "Dallas". Nevertheless, he was proceeding with his estimate.

In July, an email from Mike (major advance - we were both now "on line") informed us that Juan Alvarez had hit a problem with the new *escritura*. The *ayuntamiento* had refused permission to legally segregate the land because the plot was too small. The only way forward would be joint ownership with the new *escritura* stating that the land was owned by Antonio, Josefina and the two of us. A private agreement would then be drawn up to show which sections of the land belonged to each couple. This was not ideal and we could foresee difficulties in the future if, for example, we ever wanted to sell our half of the property. Nevertheless, without an alternative solution we accepted our lawyer's advice and emailed him to go ahead.

Hardly having recovered from this unexpected turn of events, out of the blue there came a much larger bolt: a phone call from Mister Cortijo saying that he had some unfortunate news. My heart sank. Had we lost our purchaser already? No, it was more serious than that.

"The purchaser she is happy. Very happy. Do not worry about the sale. All is going well, but I have told her not to send the remainder of the money to your *abogado*. I am worried that your money would not be safe."

"Not safe? Why ever not?"

"This is difficult for me to say, but I have been told that Juan Alvarez is bankrupt."

"Bankrupt?"

"Yes, and he was struck off the *Colegio de abogados* - this is like your Law Society - many months ago."

"You mean he is not an *abogado*."

"No, he is not an *abogado*."

"But he is still working as an *abogado*. He has an office only two floors up from the *notario*."

"This I know. It was a man in the office of the *notario* who told me. Apparently there is money owing to several people."

"And now he has our 10%."

"Yes, he has your 10%"

'I don't understand. We went with him to the *notario* only three weeks ago to get a Power of Attorney."

"This I know."

"Are you saying the *notario* knew that Juan Alvarez was no longer an *abogado*?"

"Apparently, that is correct."

"And he still approved the Power of Attorney."

"Yes."

"I don't know what to say. This could never happen in England."

"My client, she has signed the agreement and paid the full amount to her lawyer in England. The agreement signed by Juan Alvarez on your behalf will arrive any moment. Then the lawyer will send him all the money."

"But you have told your client to wait?"

"I told her there is a small problem. Nothing important. Please do not send until I call back."

"Thank goodness. But what do you suggest we do?

"You must act very quickly to find a new *abogado*."

"But how? There is no way we can come to Spain for at least two weeks. Even then, it could be days before we find an *abogado* willing to take on some other lawyer's mess."

"We do not want to lose the client, so if this is not possible, perhaps I could hold the money for you instead of Juan Alvarez. I have a copy of the agreement and you could take it yourselves to the *notario* when you come. I am never involved in the money but, if it is helpful, this time I do it."

This offer had a familiar ring. Was there not a Dutchman who once said something along similar lines? How could this be happening to us again? We had consulted a lawyer, we had signed documents in front of a notary and, theoretically, everything had been done by the book. Mister Cortijo appeared to be an honest fellow who was only trying to help, but there was no way we were prepared to put any more money at risk.

There was a possible solution. The purchaser had a British lawyer and a British bank account, so how would it be if Mister Cortijo faxed a copy of the agreement to us, we signed it and sent it to the purchaser's lawyer. The money could then be transferred into our bank account in London. Mister Cortijo readily agreed to this scheme and promised to contact his client and explain the situation.

This was accomplished and two weeks later, having rearranged our lives, we flew out to Spain. The first thing on the agenda was to take the signed sale agreement to the *notario* to be officially ratified. On the way, as it was in the same building, we paid a visit to the office of Juan Alvarez. He had stopped replying to our emails and we determined to meet him face to face and demand our money back. We were out of pocket by 668,000 pesetas, equivalent to nearly £3,000 at the time. He had pocketed the purchaser's 10% deposit on *La Caracola* plus a fee for segregation of the land we were buying in Almuñécar, about which he had done nothing.

The brass sign beside the door brazenly stating "ABOGADO" was still in place, as was his secretary who greeted us cheerily as though everything was completely normal. As for the man himself, he was absent and non-contactable. Probably, he would be in the office first thing tomorrow, but of course by the time we arrived the following morning, he had been and gone and there was no telling when he would return. We were told that he was *"muy ocupado"* (very busy).

The first thing we did in the *notario's* office was to revoke the Power of Attorney in the name of Juan Alvarez and transfer it to Mike who had agreed to keep an eye on proceedings and sign any necessary documents. The official who was dealing with our paperwork said he thought it very wise to cancel the Power of Attorney. Several other clients of Juan Alvarez had already done so. Thank you very much, we thought. You might have said something when you were charging us 7,060 pesetas to give him complete control over our affairs just a few weeks ago.

Meanwhile another official in the *notario's* office informed us that in order to ratify the purchase agreement they would need a copy of the original *escritura*. We had our copy, but the original had to be obtained from the *ayuntamiento* on the other side of town. Here we had to wait for a very long time before being informed that proof was required of the annual property tax being paid up to date. This involved finding the tax office in another part of the town and another long wait. As these local government offices were only open to the public during the mornings, by the time the tax document was handed over, the *ayuntamiento* had closed.

At the *ayuntamiento* early the following morning, an official took the copy of the property tax payments and said that they also needed proof of the land tax payments. Frustratingly, we did not have sufficient command of the language to tell the official what we thought about him and their whole shambolic and incompetent organisation. Our only recourse was to head for the nearest café and order cups of strong Spanish coffee plus, for me, a large brandy to help it down. Then, back to join the group of people waiting to be seen at the tax office before returning to join a similar crowd at the *ayuntamieno*. By closing time at 2.00 p.m. we hopefully had enough paperwork to satisfy the *notario*. But, of course, their office was now closed too.

It was on the third morning of this particular Quest that we were finally ushered into the presence of the *notario*. Quickly realising that our knowledge of Spanish was very basic, he refused to proceed on the grounds that we needed to fully understand what we were signing. A minion, summoned by telephone, escorted us out of the office and told us to wait in the corridor. A little while later, he reappeared accompanied by a woman who introduced herself in English as our translator.

Once more seated in front of the *notario,* we had to listen while the woman translated and read aloud not only the sale agreement, but the *escritura* and all the other documents we had collected. When asked, we confirmed that everything was understood and agreed. Finally satisfied, the *notario* nodded and got busy with the signing and stamping routine.

The documents were sent to the purchaser's solicitor in England and the sale of *La Caracola* was finalised in November 2001. We heard later that Mister Cortijo had been very helpful to the new owner, even visiting Los Tablones a couple of times to talk to the Difficult Neighbour about access to the water pump.

Taking into account the various fees and the 668,000 pesetas misappropriated by Juan Alvarez, the money we received was pretty well what the house had cost, including all the extra building work. No profit, but on the other hand, no loss. Subsequently, we did instruct another lawyer to recover the money owed by Juan Alvarez, but without success.

Before returning to the UK, we had to move our belongings and a few pieces of furniture that were not included in the sale, to the property in Almuñécar. Antonio had agreed we could store everything in the outbuilding next to the house. An English "Man with a Van" was located in Nerja and two strapping young men arrived the following day. Both in their early to mid twenties, they had moved from Frome in Somerset a couple of years before and were making a reasonable living, mainly from British property owners of whom there were a considerable number in and around Nerja. It was a beautiful day, the sun was shining, the scenery was fantastic, and I was a little envious of the lifestyle these two young entrepreneurs had chosen. I asked one of them how he enjoyed living in this beautiful country. He pondered for a while, giving due consideration to the question, then replied in his flat Somerset accent:

"Well, it's better than Frome."

This has become a favourite saying. Whenever something marvelous or exciting has occurred, one of us might say "That's great, isn't it?" and the other will inevitably reply dourly: "Well, it's better than Frome".

Thus ended a crazy adventure creating our own special place in the sun. An adventure, despite all the dramas, we would not have missed for the world. A few sad farewells were said to our beautiful little *cortijo*, but without too many regrets as we were looking forward to the fun of building something even more special in Almuñécar. This time, with an English-speaking builder capable of handling all the local problems, plus a little more money in hand, the creation of our new *cortijo* was going to be a stress-free and enjoyable experience.

Some people never learn, do they?

Final view on leaving

PART TWO

ALMUÑÉCAR

CHAPTER TWENTY-FOUR
This Time We Know What We Are Doing

Now that Juan Alvarez was out of the picture, we had no lawyer but, as the property was to be jointly owned, it was decided that Antonio Enrique de Weert Waltravens should act for all of us in organising the *escritura de propiedad* and the private agreement for the segregation of the land. This, of course, all took time and it was not until May 2002, nine months later, that Mike, on our behalf, signed an application for the *escritura*. A little while later, we flew out to sign the private agreement. This entailed all four parties to the agreement waiting around for most of the morning in the *notario's* office until he was free to perform the signing and stamping.

Nothing happened for another two months and then we received an email from Mike saying that the planning office at the *ayuntamiento* had now decreed that the minimum area of land required for building a house of 100m^2 was not 2,500m^2 as previously stated, but 7,000m^2. In addition, any new house had to fit exactly on to the footprint of the old one. With this unexpected bombshell all our plans and costings flew out the window. Goodbye 'Southfork'. Hello tiny cottage.

I set about trying to squeeze a kitchen, living room, dining area and bathroom into an area measuring 5.8m x 8.5m (19ft x 28ft). This meant that the bedroom would be in the low ceilinged store below.

Having designed the interiors of two houseboats, the process of juggling interior walls to find the best use of space was very similar. We decided to go for the traditional *cortijo* look. The dimensions of the main living room were based on *La Caracola* with a *chiminea* feature at one end. Although the doors and windows were in different locations and the sloping beamed ceiling was a little bit higher, it should have the same feel. There was no room for the traditional arched recess with the shelves and water jugs, but I found a suitable space in a small corridor outside the bathroom.

We enjoyed the coziness of the thick walls of *La Caracola* with its deep window recesses, so the plans showed the two window walls of the living room built double thickness; two 20cm wide blocks instead of one. The exception was in one corner where a spiral staircase led down to the bedroom. Here, to save space, the walls would be thinner to create a snug alcove for the stairs.

The plans were dispatched to Mike for costing. The new design would be considerably cheaper than the original and we were beginning to reconcile ourselves to having a tiny holiday home when the next bolt hit us. Mike telephoned with the devastating news that the *ayuntamiento* would not give permission for a new house on the site. They would only allow a *reforma* (restoration) of the existing building. Moreover, they would only accept plans from an architect - expensive – and, even then, it is possible that permission might not be granted. Great! All these changes of rules seemed as though they were aimed at us personally. What were we to do now?

Mike advised that the existing building was not worth restoring and suggested forgetting the whole thing for a year or two when the rules would probably have changed. That is how things happened in Spain. As far as we were concerned, this was not an option and we asked him to proceed with his estimate.

The project did have to be placed on the back burner for a while because we had decided on a huge change in our lifestyle in the UK. I had just officially retired and although clients continued to ask for exhibition designs or video production, these could be organised from anywhere we chose to live. Similarly, Alison's one-woman shows were performed throughout England and Wales, so all she needed was reasonable access to a motorway. We were free agents.

Our double-decker houseboat on Taggs Island

The London property market was booming and a pad on the river near Hampton Court, even a floating hut, had become most desirable. With the discovery that our houseboat was worth two and half times our investment, the decision to move from Taggs Island was confirmed.

We had an exploratory look at the West Country, but were disheartened by the terrible road access to almost anywhere. Then, returning one day from giving a performance in south Wales, Alison passed a sign to Ogmore-By-Sea and simply because the name appealed, went to have a look. It was a small group of houses and one shop clustered around a spectacular bay with a rocky shoreline leading to vast acres of sandy beach. Peaceful and remote, it seemed the perfect location. She had to stop at one point to let some sheep amble across the road - little different from the roads in West London - yet it was only fifteen minutes to the M4. Property prices were incredibly attractive, so we placed ourselves on the books of an agent in the nearby town of Bridgend.

We took it in turns to travel to Wales every other weekend to see if anything interesting had turned up, and one Saturday afternoon when I was working away in my office on the river Thames, Alison called from Wales (we actually had mobile phones by now). She was standing outside an isolated house high up on a hill, not at Ogmore-By-Sea but to the north of Bridgend. As the agent had only that day been instructed and was not yet in possession of the keys, she could not see inside. The reason for the call was to describe the location. Somewhat reminiscent of *La Caracola,* the house was perched high up on one side of a valley with panoramic views of the hills and, in the distance beyond Bridgend, the coastline at Ogmore-By-Sea.

The downside was that it was not the character building we had been looking for, being a typical two up two down stone Welsh farmhouse that had been extended back and front. The extensions, that more than doubled the size of the house, had been carried out without much thought and the whole lot was rendered and painted cream. There was no mains drainage and water had to be pumped from a nearby spring. The "garden" was a large area mainly consisting of waste high nettles and assorted debris. Access was from a narrow country road onto a track about two thirds of a mile long across a common. It all sounded impossible.

My reaction was to put in an offer immediately. Alison was hesitant because I had not seen the property and we had no idea what it was like inside. However, I was not concerned because of her obvious enthusiasm for the location. We would both travel to Wales the next weekend and if, for some reason, it was not a goer, we would simply withdraw the offer.

Alison returned to the agent's office and they put in a call to the vendor. The offer, some way below the asking price, was immediately accepted. Half an hour later, I received a phone call informing me that we were the proud owners of the wonderfully named "Tal-y-Fan Farm".

Meanwhile, the houseboat had been on the market for a number of weeks with the sale about to be concluded. The money we were to receive for our floating hut was a great deal more than the price of a five-bedroom house in Wales - with large garden, paddock and spectacular views.

June 2002 saw us moving from our home on the River Thames to a rented flat in Ogmore-By-Sea. The interior of the Welsh house we had bought was in such a poor state that much needed doing before we wished to move in. With funds available, we were able to upgrade the whole house including the addition of three windows to take advantage of the fabulous views.

By chance, we were recommended a wonderful Welsh builder called Wilf when talking to the landlord of the local pub-restaurant. He arranged for us to meet Wilf there the following morning. When the introductions had been completed and we were ready to go up to the house, we were surprised when the landlord asked us to hang on while he got his coat. We asked Wilf why he was he coming too. Wilf did not seem to think this particularly odd and explained: "Well, he's Welsh and he's nosey".

Not only did the landlord come and have a good look round, but he expressed forceful opinions about what we should and should not be doing to improve the house; some of which we took on board, others we did not.

*

Meanwhile, we had almost forgotten that Mike was supposed to be sending us a quotation for building the Spanish house. Nothing had been heard for several weeks, so I sent him an email. His reply stated that he was very sorry for the delay, but could do nothing at the moment because he had parked outside a client's house on a windy day and a palm tree had blown down, completely crushing the front of his car. Unfortunately, his brief case containing our plans, was on the front seat. Could we send copies please?

I emailed back saying that we had heard some good excuses in our time, but this one took the biscuit. I had to swallow my words when he sent a photograph of his car with the front end absolutely flattened by the tree.

At the beginning of December, we left Wilf and his two assistants knocking down walls and installing a new kitchen and bathroom in Wales while we made a seven-day trip to check what progress, if any, there had been in Spain.

Mike had still not prepared any costings, preferring to wait for some official plans from an architect. To this end, he had set up a meeting with a technical architect, a pleasant lady called Luciana, who was preparing the *proyecto reforma* (plan for restoring the existing building). This plan, to be sent to Madrid for registration, showed the exterior only with the proposed positions for new windows. Hopefully, she would receive the accepted plans by the end of January. They then had to be taken to the planning department at the *ayuntamiento* for approval. This could take another 4-6 weeks, so it would be well into March before we could start building.

Although we were requesting permission for a *reforma*, her proposal was to knock down the existing building. This, of course, was entirely illegal, but Luciana said she would take photos of the walls to show how bad they were and if the *ayuntamiento* discovered what we were up to, she would do a report stating that the walls were dangerous and had to be replaced.

Once again, we were becoming involved in something that felt unnecessarily dodgy, but Mike said that this was quite normal practice in Spain and even if the *ayuntamiento* decided to levy a fine, it would not be very onerous. So we paid Luciana 1,000 euros (half her fee) to proceed. The peseta had been replaced by the euro just a few months before on the 1st January 2002. Suddenly, everything seemed to cost more money than when we were handing out huge quantities of fairy-tale pesetas.

The next visit was to the *abogado* Waltravens to see if he had sorted out the all-important *escritura*. He had not. What on earth had he been doing for the past six months? His explanation was that there had been "problems", but he was working on it.

There was little point in travelling up into the hills to look at the site. Nothing had been done. All the same, we needed confirmation that our investment was as good as we remembered and still worthwhile pursuing. It was with great relief that we both found it a jewel of a place and somewhere we wished to spend our time.

However, as we drove up, we were gob-smacked to see a brand new house on our neighbour's section of the land. How was this possible? We were told that planning permission took months, so how on earth could Antonio and Josefina build on our jointly owned land even before the *escritura* had been ratified? Perhaps there is one law for the Spanish and another for foreigners. Or perhaps the Spaniards just get on and do what they want and worry about the bureaucracy later.

Then a devastating thought occurred. If the land is officially only large enough for one 50m² house and Waltravens had somehow managed to register Antonio's new house, could we ever obtain permission for ours?

It was clear that an English-peaking lawyer had to be found to look after our interests. But where to look? First stop was the tourist information office in Almuñécar who produced the name of a likely *abogado*. His office, with a sign stating that English, German, Danish and Dutch was spoken here, was sensibly placed on the sea front near the big tourist hotels. The smart young *abogado* who greeted us, listened attentively to our tale of woe and asked a few pertinent questions. He pondered for a short while and then declared that we had found ourselves in an interesting situation that he, personally - no offence - would not touch with a bargepole (or words to that effect). Wishing us every success in a tone suggesting he thought this an unlikely outcome, he rose and shook us both by the hand, indicating that the interview was over.

The final straw on this not very successful week was when we reminded Mike that he had not given us an invoice for his time and expenses. This, he admitted, was because he had lost all his notes. Could we possibly supply a record of what he had done for us during the past two years? Oh, and by the way, he had given up being a builder as he was now making a better living advising and assisting foreigners who wished to build or rent in the town of Salobreña.

To sum up, we still had no *escritura* to prove that we were joint owners of the land and no permission to build although, seemingly against all the rules, the other party to the agreement had already built a house on the land; our technical architect was seeking planning permission to renovate our existing building when her actual intention was to demolish it; we no longer had faith in the *abogado* who was also being instructed by the other party, but we had failed to find an English-speaking replacement to sort out the muddle. To top it all, in the rapidly receding likelihood of a favourable solution to all of the above, we no longer had a builder.

Oh hell!

CHAPTER TWENTY-FIVE
Progress

JANUARY 2003 - Wales

Good news! An email from Luciana stating that she had received the approval of the *proyecto reforma* from Madrid and had taken it to the *ayuntamiento*. We should receive our *licencia de obras* (planning permission) within two or three weeks. The building process could then start - assuming we could find a builder. The two or three weeks stretched to more than three months and it was April when Mike told us that the *licencia de obras* had finally arrived. He pointed out, as if we did not know, that things often take a long time in Spain.

Finding a builder was now a priority.

More good news! As luck would have it, some friends of ours, Denise and Martin, had purchased a house a year or so before in the village of Maro on the outskirts of Nerja and were happy to recommend their English speaking *abogado* - or, as she was female, *abogada*. Isabella spoke fluent English and her office in Nerja was only thirty minutes drive from Almuñécar.

A meeting was arranged by email for the day after we were next due in Spain. Meanwhile, our main preoccupation was the move from Ogmore-By-Sea into the Welsh house that Wilf had so splendidly renovated.

MAY 2003 - Spain for 7 days

We met the abogada, Isabella. In contrast to the dingy atmosphere of Waltraven's cramped office, here there was space and light and walls lined with large framed posters of art exhibitions from Spain, Paris and London depicting famous paintings from a variety of artists. We later discovered that she likes to visit the art scene in the capital cities as frequently as possible.

The lady herself was an attractive woman in her early forties. The navy blue dress hugging her slim figure was surely from Paris or London and her shoulder-length black hair had a stylish cut that would pass muster in Knightsbridge. A diamond ring and gold bracelet occasionally caught the light. Subtle make-up completed the elegant image.

The explanation of our predicament did not produce the negative reaction experienced with our last English-speaking *abogado.*

"This will take some unraveling, mm? But it is not unusual. I have many British and Scandinavian clients with similar situations, mm?"

Her grasp of English and her accent were both perfect, but she had a habit of adding an interrogative "mm?" to the end of sentences, as if to ensure that we were keeping up.

"The first thing we do is make a call to this Waltravens to find out what is happening about your *escritura de propiedad* and tell him that I am now representing you, mm? Let us do that now."

During the phone call, she raised her eyebrows at us a few times indicating that she was not impressed with what she was hearing. Eventually, with a sigh, she replaced the receiver.

"This Waltravens has done nothing to obtain the new *escritura*. This is important, mm? He says that your friend - Mike, is it? - has lost all his papers including the Power of Attorney so nothing can be signed. Fortunately, we do not have to register the house separately as it is only a *reforma*. The existing house will be included in the original *escritura*. If we had to register a new house, that would be another whole complication. It can all be sorted out. In Spain there is always a way, mm?"

This was all very heartening and following Isabella's advice, we obtained a copy of the Power of Attorney from the office of the *notorio* and delivered it to Waltraven's office. Thus, Mike could sign the *escritura* as soon as it was drawn up.

We visited Martin and Denise, who happened to be staying in their house in Maro at the time, and thanked them for introducing us to Isabella. Hearing that we were looking for a builder, Denise suggested the man they used to "reform" their own house. She said that Rafael had done a splendid job for them and, what is more, he is incredibly dishy. Alison agreed that this was a serious consideration when choosing your workmen. Our Welsh builder, Wilf, had certainly passed the test.

We were amused to hear that although their property was an imposing two-storey town house, Rafael had been most unhappy with the state of the walls. It was a listed building so they only had permission for a *reforma*, but this did include replacing the roof. However, once the roof timbers had been removed - wouldn't you know it? - the walls collapsed. Nobody saw them go and Rafael denied giving them a push. This was heartening to hear, considering Luciana's intentions for our own *reforma*.

The following day there was a meeting with Rafael in Maro where I showed him my plans. Although he spoke no English, he was quick to catch on to the traditional style of building envisaged. As with Eddie, he completely understood our wish for rough plastered walls, ceilings with rounded beams (even if cosmetic) and a look that was *rustico*. The idea of "accidentally" knocking down the house was of no consequence to him, so long as Luciana was responsible for informing the authorities. We left it that he would prepare an all-in price and post it to us in the UK.

We heard that a motorway was being built from east to west of Spain along the south coast and were concerned that it might come close to our new house. We enquired at the *ayuntamiento* and eventually found a man with a map. The route had not been finalised, but our plot was so high up that, if the motorway did come through our valley, it would be a long way down. We decided not to worry.

DECEMBER 2003 - Spain for 9 days
At a meeting with Mike and Rafael, we approved Rafael's meticulously detailed quotation and signed a contract. Without a *deposito* and any means of filling it, water was going to be a problem. As a temporary arrangement during the building process, Antonio agreed to run a hose down from his *deposito* and charge us for the amount of water used. In the future, when Rafael had built us our own *deposito*, Antonio proposed that we should share his water rights. When the time came, it only needed Antonio to sign an authorisation.

A visit to see our new abogada, Isabella, and we were hardly knocked off our feet when informed that our Dutch friend, Mr Waltravens, had failed to organise our *escritura*.

"I spoke to him on the telephone last week. I wanted to know what he was doing. The man was doing nothing, mm? So I have taken it over myself. We won't have to deal with him any more. I will get the *escritura* ratified. I cannot see any problem but, of course, it will take a little time."

Well, there's a surprise.

We mentioned our lack of electricity at the property and the fact that the supply company, visited several times, was being far from helpful. Isabella explained that we had been visiting a retail supplier who was probably not keen to lay cables up in the hills. There were other companies who specialised in this kind of work and she would contact someone she knew.

FEBRUARY 2004 – Spain for 6 days

Up until now, we had been booking hotels in Almuñécar for our trips but, now that it was up and running, Martin and Denise had kindly offered us the use of their house in Maro. With somewhere pleasant to stay, it made life much more civilized and we continued to take advantage of their splendid establishment until we could move in to our own home.

Rafael had been on site for several weeks and we are eager to see what he had done. We travelled up to the house – and it was not there! Instead there was an enormous hole in the ground. The attractive arches had disappeared as they were in the way of the digging machine. Just the store was left standing. Rafael had made the hole lower

Large hole where the house had been

Steps beside the wine store

than the original – not strictly allowed by the planners – so that the bedroom would have a decent head height. He suggested cutting back into the hillside to increase the size of the bedroom. Definitely not allowed by the planners, but who is going to notice? With this extra space, I asked if we could include a small shower room. Rafael, as always, saw no problem so we measured up the space so that when we arrived home, I could design a layout and send him the new plans.

With Isabella in charge, Mike had ceased to be involved. We were very grateful for his help and he, no doubt, was very grateful to be well out of it.

APRIL 2004 – Spain for 5 days

The little *deposito* had been built. It held 10,000 litres, which we felt, was quite enough for our needs. Antonio came with us to talk to *el presidente* at the *comunidad de regantes* about tapping into the supply pipe on his land and adding a stopcock to give us our own water. All seems to be proceeding well until the man enquired about the size of our *deposito.* Upon hearing the answer, the form he had been filling in was crumpled up and thrown into the waste paper bin. The shortest amount of time they can turn on the water from their big pipe was a quarter of an hour. This would provide around 17,500 litres and as our *deposito* only held 10,000 litres it was not possible to have a connection to their system.

After some lengthy discussion and a lot of shrugging and sighing, they came up with an alternative solution. Antonio was not very happy, but he signed an authorisation to have our supply of water put into his *deposito.* The arrangement being that every 17,500 litres we bought would be put into his *deposito* and he would then fill our 10,000 litre tank. Thus, he would gain 7,500 litres of water each time for his trouble, but we felt this is a price worth paying.

It only remained for Rafael to organise the stopcock at Antonio's tank with a permanent pipe running down to our *deposito.* Meanwhile, Antonio would continue filling our tank with his hose.

In the little village of Maro, Alison noticed a sign advertising, among other things, electric underfloor heating. It was a bit of a novelty at that time, especially in Spain, but Wilf had installed it in the kitchen and bathroom of our Welsh house and it worked beautifully. Even so, I thought

Alison beside the new *deposito*

it a complete waste of money to consider such a system in Spain. Alison reminded me that the temperature dropped during the long dark evening in November/December when we intended to be here, and insisted on investigating.

The company was owned by a Danish couple with Hanna, the wife, running the office. It was all extremely efficient. We handed over a copy of our plans and two days later were presented with a set of drawings showing all the cable runs. It was a very reasonable price and I was persuaded to go ahead. Hanna said we could leave everything to them. She would liaise with Rafael, who lived a couple of streets away, and agree a schedule for the installation. When we eventually moved into the house, Alison was proved right. Warm floors in the evenings during the Winter months were a very pleasant luxury.

JUNE 2004 – Spain for 7 days
Great excitement! The first sight of our new house. It was the same shape as the original building but much more solid. The main difference was a strong flat roof at the front of the house where, one day, we hoped to build a second floor bedroom; this was, if the people at the *ayuntamiento* ever relaxed their planning restrictions. Our immediate concern was that with the grey cement walls, it all looked worryingly stark.

Inside, the dividing walls had all been built although not yet rendered with cement. This would happen after the plumbing and electrical wiring had been installed. The idea of making the walls only 20cm thick in the spiral staircase corner worked a treat. The stairs, a triumph of brickwork construction, fitted snugly into the alcove.

Moving down to the bedroom, with the standard height ceiling and the increased floor area, there was now plenty of room for a king-size bed and two built-in cupboards. Even the little shower room did not seem at all cramped. Rafael was obviously pleased with how it was all working out and we expressed our gratitude and delight.

JULY 2004 – Spain for 7 days
Our *abogada,* as promised, had contacted an electrical contractor. His name was Alfonso and he wanted to explain the problems and agree a price. So, once gain, we were on our way to Spain.

Expecting our electrician to be wearing T-shirt and jeans and turn up in a van, we were somewhat surprised when a smart Mercedes arrived at the house. The trim little man who got out had sleek black hair, small moustache and glasses, and was formally dressed in suit and tie. He was carrying a large black leather briefcase. This was evidently not a man who got his hands dirty and, immediately, we started worrying about money.

With his few words of English and Alison's tenuous grasp of Spanish, we were able to gather that he had spoken to the *Sevillana* (private electricity company) and there was no nearby connection available. This meant bringing an aerial cable from the nearest transformer some way down the valley up to a new pole with a meter, all of which we would have to pay for. From the pole to the house, more than a quarter of a mile, an armoured cable would have to be buried under the road with several inspection manholes along the way. But first, permission must be sought from neighbours whose land would be under the aerial cable. He would also have to obtain authorization from the *ayuntamiento* and permission from the *Sevillana*. He was convinced that all the permissions could be achieved within a few days, following which he would send us a final quotation. It all sounded incredibly expensive - which, indeed, it was. When we received his quotation, it amounted to only a little less than we had paid Antonio for the entire property. Electricity was vital, so there was little alternative other than to swallow hard and accept the inevitable.

First view of new house

House from the north-west

Spiral staircase from bedroom

Living room with door to balcony

Rafael with Alison

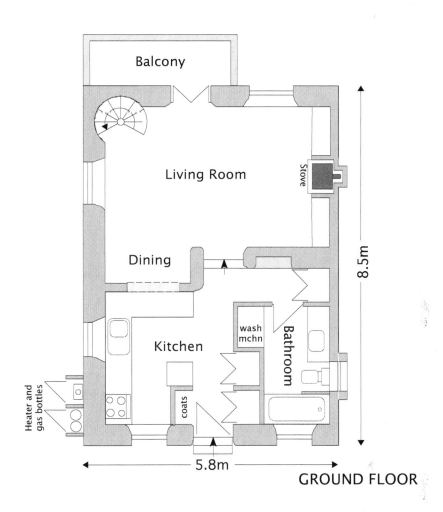

Balcony

Living Room

Stove

Dining

wash mchn

Kitchen

Bathroom

coats

Heater and gas bottles

8.5m

5.8m

GROUND FLOOR

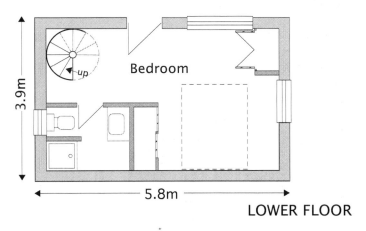

Bedroom

up

3.9m

5.8m

LOWER FLOOR

159

SEPTEMBER 2004 – Spain for 9 days

Our fifth trip to Spain this year. The costs of flights and hire car fees were mounting up. Isabella needed us to sign the new *escritura de propiedad* in front of the *notario* with Antonio and Josefina. This Title Deed was to be sent to Madrid for registration, which could take up to two months, and then the joint ownership of the land would be official.

Rafael had fitted heavy Spanish-style wooden doors and windows. Although we had lost some internal space by specifying 40cm thick walls, the deep windows sills provided the old *cortijo* look we had hoped for. It was all incredibly pleasing.

Alfonso arrived in his Mercedes to show us the cables that were now buried in the road from the pole to the house. The new pole with its meter had been erected, but the cable was not yet strung across the valley to the substation. He promised to sort this out during the next two or three weeks.

Everything was looking good. Once the electricity was connected and Rafael had left the site, we could apply for the *licencia de primera ocupación* which is granted when a building has been completed and approved according to the *licencia de obras* (planning permission). As soon as this was received, we could move in. It had taken three long years to get to this point but, at last, the end was in sight.

CHAPTER TWENTY-SIX
Everything Stops

NOVEMBER 2004 - Wales

An email arrived from our project architect, Luciana, saying she has been issued with a notification to stop all work because we had violated the *licencia de obras* by a) knocking down the original house, b) building a second floor below thereby increasing the floor area beyond 50m², and c) digging up the road for an electric cable. We had, of course, done all these things, but how did the *ayuntamiento* know? The most likely explanation is that someone locally had "denounced" us - a nasty habit left over from General Franco's time.

Luciana is going to explain that the original building was unsafe and the lower floor was there already (not mentioning that it is now a bit bigger). Furthermore, Alfonso, the electrician, did speak to the relevant department in the *ayuntamiento* before digging up the road.

We had hardly recovered from this when we received a telephone call from Isabella. She had never called us in England before so we immediately feared the worst, although she did sound quite upbeat.

"I thought you would like to know that I have just received your *escritura* from Madrid. You are now the official joint owners of the land with your neighbours. Mm? You can come and collect it any time."

Great, we now owned the plot, but we were not allowed to finish our house. A short while later, another email arrived from Luciana. The *ayuntamiento* accepted that the building had been unsafe but did not accept that the new building was 62m² rather than the 50m² allowed. We must pay a fine or we cannot continue to build. How much was this going to cost us?

The fine was based on the percentage of the additional size of the building, i.e. 12m², which Luciana had calculated to be less than 300 euros. Wow! Relief all round. We put a cheque in the post immediately.

MARCH 2005 - Spain for 10 days

We could hardly contain our excitement. At the end of January - fantastic news - the building work had been completed. Rafael had cleared up and left the site.

Driving up the track from the riverbed and rounding the final corner, the sight of our dream home, newly painted and gleaming white in the sunshine, seemed to be welcoming us.

There was a concrete pad to park our car just outside the wire mesh security fence, which though necessary, was not a thing of beauty. Hopefully, one day it would be covered with vines and other greenery.

Once inside the house, we were immediately struck by how the doors, windows and round ceiling beams, all stained a dark walnut, featured so richly against the white of the ceilings and walls. And because of the high ceilings and open design, there was an unexpected feeling of space. The small kitchen did not seem at all cramped. There was masses of work surface, all tiled white, and the fridge, freezer and oven were all neatly tucked away exactly as planned.

The living room especially, with its traditional fireplace feature and double doors leading on to a balcony, seemed impossibly large for such a tiny house. In the corner of the room, the *escalera de caracol* (spiral staircase) leading down to the bedroom was a triumph with its tiled treads and dark timber nosings. I congratulated Rafael on the wonderful curved cement work, calling it an "escalera Rolls Royce". He replied:

Non, escalera Ferrari!

The bedroom itself was another space larger than we could have imagined. We loved the Spanish style doors to the shower room and the two fitted cupboards. Another chunky door led out onto the lower terrace with the orange and lemon trees. The shower room with white floor, blue and yellow patterned wall tiles and dark blue shower cubicle was another triumph, as was the bathroom up on the ground floor.

We wandered around, pointing out features and hugging ourselves with delight. The whole house, to us, was like a jewel and we could not wait to live in it. Now that the building has been completed, we should be able to apply for the *licencia de primera ocupación*. Then, all we have to do is organise the electricity and gas.

The next day, full of optimism, we made an appointment to see Isabella. First item on the list was to collect the *escritura de propiedad* and pay her bill to date, which was surprisingly little. Now that we officially owned the land, we assumed that we had all the documentation we needed to get on with our lives. But no.

"There is a problem with the registration of the house, mm? I have been informed that the old house does not exist in the records of the *ayuntamiento*. Therefore, we have to apply to get your new house registered. This could take a little while."

"But this is nonsense. Antonio has confirmed that the building was registered when he built it and he even has receipts for the rates he paid over a number of years. Can you not go back to them with this proof?"

"I am afraid that is not how things work here. If the *ayuntamiento* say there are no records then there is nothing we can do about it. I have to go to see the Registrar to register your home as a new house, mm? And then take the document to be notorised. This will then be sent to Granada for ratification."

"How can they say the house doesn't exist? We have photos taken back in 2000 before we bought it and, of course, they have given us permission to reform it!"

"I know. This doesn't seem reasonable. But they insist there are no records. What can I say? Until this has been sorted, you will not be granted the *licencia de primera ocupación,* the *Sevillana* will not connect the electricity and you cannot live in the house. I am sorry, but this has to be done. It is important. Yes?"

Isabella gave us a list of documents required to accompany the registration application and many hours were spent putting them all together and making copies. Included were plans of the house, the original *licencia de obras* (planning permission), the *Certificado final de la direción de la obra* (certificate of completion of work from Ima), and copies of all our bank statements showing how much money we had brought into the country. I even had to take photos of the house from all sides.

It took two full days before everything was collated and neatly clipped into a file. Triumphantly, we delivered it to Isabella, imagining that we could now relax. But no.

"What I now have to do is prepare a *certificado catastro* (a certificate for the annual land tax). We will declare the cost of the land at the official price paid of 12,000 euros."

"How much tax will that mean?"

"For the land, you will have to pay an annual amount of 48 euros."

"Oh well, that's not too bad."

"But that is for the land only. The annual tax on the house is separate. I will have to prepare a Form 901 declaring the rateable value of the house based upon the cost of the building, mm? For this, I am going to need all the receipts and a complete breakdown of costs."

There was a pause while we took this in.

"This is not turning out to be a very relaxing holiday for you, is it?"

Another load of forms and certificates and another session with the *notorio* to witness signatures.

Three days ago we thought everything was going fine. Now it was turning into some sort of nightmare. Desperately in need of a break, we travelled to Velez Malaga to burden our friends Roger and Pepe with our problems. They had finished upgrading their house which, of course, looked superb. During the five years or more since we had last visited, the garden had matured into a riot of exotic trees, shrubs and cacti. We were very full of admiration.

Back at the house, the electrical contractor, Alphonso, came to demonstrate that his work had been completed. He showed us the fuse box in the house with its rows of trip switches (more than we had in our five-bedroom house in Wales) and we then trudged up the track to inspect our meter fixed to the new pole, at the top of which was a heavy cable looping down and across the valley to some far distant pole. On the way back to the house, Alphonso proudly pointed out four manhole covers along the road for access to the cable that had been run underground. We were informed that it had taken machinery, men and a great deal of time to do this work. All very impressive, but we never understood why our cable had to be installed in such an extraordinarily complicated way. Every other house in the area had a wire running from a nearby pole.

The one thing that Alphonso was not able to demonstrate was the electricity actually working. In order to have our electricity switched on, it was necessary to provide the *Sevillana* with copies of all the forms Isabella had sent to Granada plus the *licencia de primera ocupación*. Be that as it may, Alphonso had fulfilled his contract and we duly wrote him a huge cheque. This he placed in his big black brief case. We shook hands and assumed that this was the last we would see of him.

Meanwhile, we decided to purchase some Calor gas bottles so that we could have hot water. At least this was something positive that could be organised before returning to the UK. At the office in the town square opposite the dreaded *ayuntamiento,* we explained to the grim-faced woman behind the counter that we would like to buy two bottles please. The puzzled expression that crossed her face suggested that nobody had ever entered the Calor gas shop before and asked such an extraordinary question.

"I cannot sell you gas bottles. We have to inspect your installation. I have to make an appointment for our engineer to visit your house."

"But this is a new house and we have an official certificate of installation from our plumber."

"You cannot have gas until we have looked at the installation. I will make an appointment for you now."

Of course, they were "very busy", so we had to wait a week for the visitation when the man, after only a cursory glance at our water heater, expressed himself satisfied. It was installed in a *casita* (small brick house) built onto the outside wall of the kitchen as per regulations. That evening, brandishing the form of approval the man had given us, we returned to the office and demanded our two bottles.

"I need to see your passports".

We always carried them - in case.

"And your NIE numbers."

"Yes, we have those too."

"And I need a copy of your licencia de obras (planning permission) and three copies of the plumbers installation certificate."

Why on earth could she not have said all this the first time we walked in? However, we returned the following morning, via the photocopy shop, and presented the forms. Could we please have our bottles now?

"It is necessary to make an appointment for an engineer to deliver the bottles and make the connection. I will make an appointment for you now."

Four more days passed until the appointed hour when a battered white van arrived driven by a small worried looking man in brown overalls. He produced two gas bottles from the back of the van and carried them to the waiting *casita*. Speedily, he fitted to the water heater a length of rubber hose with, on the other end, a fitment to clamp on to a gas bottle. Job done, or so we thought. Then he demanded:

"I need to see your primera ocupación."

"Our licencia de primera ocupación?"

"Yes".

"Sorry, we do not have it at the moment."

"You do not have a licencia de primera ocupación?"

"Not yet. Our abogada is organising it. We will have it very soon."

Although "very soon" was, perhaps, stretching a point, it cut no ice with this important little man. Without saying a word, he produced a penknife, cut the hose he had just fitted, grabbed the two bottles, marched back to his van, and drove off.

No electricity - and now no gas!

The whole episode was so ridiculous that we just stood there and laughed as the van disappeared down the track in a cloud of dust.

Following a recuperative cup of tea, we shut up the house and returned to where we were staying in Maro. It had become perfectly clear that there was no point in worrying about anything until Isabella had sorted out the registration of the house. So, for the remaining two days of our stay, we determined to relax and enjoy the sunshine.

JULY 2005 - Spain for 10 days
Nearly four months had passed since all the paperwork had been sent to Granada, but when we visited Isabella we could tell by the look on her face that all was not well.

"There is a complication with registering your house. The piece of land you jointly own is only big enough for one 50m^2 building and Antonio has already his house. They say there cannot be another house on this land."

"But there is another house. We have built it!"

"Of course. I have explained to the Registrar that there definitely is a house. I have seen it, mm? What is more, I have given them copies of all the permissions from the *ayuntamiento* including the approval of the completed building. I cannot believe how stupid they are being. And they have now come back with a request for more information."

Not satisfied with the bank statements confirming how much money we brought into the country, they were demanding a letter from the bank stating that to the best of their knowledge all the money was solely for the reform of our house. This entailed a tedious session with the bank manager, taking up an entire morning, who was not at all keen to put his name to this *Declaration de Inversion*. After all, how did he know what we had spent the money on?

But there was more. They had a copy of our *escritura de propiedad* and although it had been signed by Antonio, Josefina and the two of us in front of a *notorio,* we were directed to sign another document in front of a *notorio* confirming that we had indeed all signed the original.

Our neighbours, once again, were cooperative and extremely patient. It was all a great waste of their time, but they stoically accepted that this was the way officialdom functioned in Spain.

167

Isabella, who had accompanied us to the *notorio,* was now confident that she had all the documentation needed to register the house.

"We should have approval in two or three weeks. To save time, we should go now to the *ayuntamiento* and prepare an application form for your *licencia de primera ocupación*. Without this licence you cannot connect your electricity."

We had visited the *ayuntamiento* in Motril many times when trying to solve problems with *La Caracola,* but this one in Almuñecar was new to us. An imposing traditional style building painted yellow and white, it was situated in the main square just down from the cathedral in the old part of the town. All around the square colourful chairs and tables were set out in front of several cafes.

Once inside, it felt like any other modern municipal building. White tiled floors, white walls and a grand marble staircase leading to long corridors lined with doors on each floor. Isabella led the way to the planning office on the third floor. She asked us to wait outside while she went in to see if anyone was available to attend to us. She emerged a few moments later, saying that we had to wait a while. This was expected. Waiting is what we did. After a while, the door was opened and a man carrying a briefcase and a roll of plans marched grimly out of the office - another satisfied customer - and Isabella ushered us in.

It is a large rectangular room with walls lined with filing cabinets and shelves with even more files. Behind four large desks men are silently writing or shuffling papers. Hunched behind one of these desks is a diminutive sour-faced man with a pointed nose and untidy grey hair. He is dressed in a rumpled grey suit with a green tie sitting askew in an equally rumpled shirt collar. A cigarette hung from the corner of his mouth. He studiously ignored us for some time as he busied himself with stuffing papers into a file before dumping it on to one of several stacks of files on his desk. Only then did he look up and acknowledge our presence.

Isabella introduced us to Paco, the man whose aim in life was seemingly to find ways of delaying the completion of our paperwork. Paco listened with a bored expression on his face, the fingers of his right hand tapping the desk impatiently, as Isabella brought him up to date on our progress ending with a request for an application form for the *licencia de primera ocupación*. Reluctantly the man stirred himself and, opening a drawer in his desk, produced the application form.

Summing up for us, Isabella explained that she would fill in the application and as soon as the Form 901 was returned from Granada with the rateable value of our house, Paco would issue the *licencia de primera ocupación*. There was the possibility of a delay (of course) as he might have to send a man to visit the property again. He could not possibly say at the moment.

We took our leave and all headed for the nearest cafe and restorative coffees. It seemed like all this bureaucratic nonsense was going on forever. Antonio had built a house on our jointly owned land some three years before and at the same time our friends, Martin and Denise, had built theirs in Maro; so why were we having all these problems? Isabella tried to explain.

"There is a lot of confusion since Spain joined the European Union. Rules are changing every day as they try to move from the old, corrupt, ways of doing things to implement EU regulations. It is a new way of thinking, mm?"

As a joke, we suggested that Isabella should bribe someone to get our paperwork sorted. Her reply was an eye-opener.

"Yes, I have considered this, but I am based in Nerja. I know everybody there. I understand how the system works. The problem in Almuñécar is that I do not know the right people."

We nodded sympathetically, but thought it best not to pursue the subject.

CHAPTER TWENTY-SEVEN
The House Does Not Exist!

AUGUST 2005 - Wales

Isabella emailed to say that there had been another hold-up because Granada wanted Luciana to witness her own signature in front of the *notario* on the planning permission *(licencia de obras)* that she had signed in front of the *notorio* two years previously! Unfortunately, Luciana was on holiday. More delays.

Three weeks later we phoned Isabella who said she still had not been able to contact Luciana. More delays.

SEPTEMBER 2005 - Wales

We waited another three weeks before phoning again and this time Isabella confirmed that Luciana had been to the *notario* and witnessed her signature. She had not yet collected the document and send it to Granada, but would do so later in the week. Still more delays. Then came another one of those alarming phone calls from Isabella.

"I have talked to the people in the Registry Office, mm? - and they are refusing to register your house. They are still saying the piece of land you jointly own is only big enough for one house. Therefore, there cannot possibly be another house on that land."

"But this is crazy. We have been through all this."

"I know. It is mad. I have sent them copies of the permission from the *ayuntamiento* to rebuild the house and the final approval of the building. Even photos. I will have to find some way to get them to accept this. It is vital for you, mm? At the moment your house does not exist."

Four and half long years had gone by since we had bought the Spanish property and six months since Rafael had finished building the house, which apparently does not exist. There seemed to be no end in sight. The highs and lows along the journey had somehow evened themselves out, but now, for the first time, a deep depression set in. We wanted shot of the whole project. We hated the Spanish and never wanted to visit their wretched country again. Various ways of selling up were considered, but without the house being registered this was not feasible. No one would buy it. And then there was the problem of the joint ownership. Everything legal had to be agreed and signed by our neighbours. There was nothing for it, we simply had to pull ourselves together and press on.

OCTOBER 2005 - Spain for 4 days

There was no news for the following few weeks, so we decided to fly out for a brief visit to rattle a few cages. Thanks to the generosity of our friends, we were able to stay in the Maro house once more, convenient for visiting Isabella at her office in nearby Nerja.

There was little point in traveling to Almuñécar to see our property as it could only make us more depressed. Nevertheless, we felt it our duty to go and check that it was still in one piece and had not slithered down the hillside.

Later when relaxing on the terrace soaking up the sunshine, Alison remarked: "Just look at those hills and mountains. You could not possibly buy that view". Except, of course, we had! Our enthusiasm was definitely rekindled. Whatever barriers were to be placed in our way, this was worth fighting for - only we were not expecting to face another barrier quite so quickly.

When we telephoned Isabella the next day, she told us that all the paperwork had been delivered to the *ayuntamiento* as requested, but she had been informed that this was not sufficient. The man we were dealing with, Paco, now referred to as the Annoying Little Git, had decreed that the *licencia de primera ocupación* could not be completed without a certificate from the *Sevillana* stating that we do not have electricity. He also demanded another certificate from the town water company stating that we do not have mains water supply.

Isabella could not explain why they required this information or what it had to do with the licence. The people in the *ayuntamiento* would know perfectly well that nobody had mains water in the hills. Indeed, some of them, or their relatives, would own houses up there themselves. Similarly, it was equal nonsense to prove that the *Sevillana* was not supplying electricity when they were not allowed to switch it on until we had our *licencia de primera ocupación.*

It was no surprise then, when the people at the water company were totally nonplussed. We did not have water, we were not customers of theirs and they did not feel disposed to write letters or issue certificates on the subject. All too aware of our pathetic inability to speak the language, they suggested that we had misunderstood what the *ayuntamiento* wanted.

171

We were more successful at the office of the *Sevillana*. After waiting for our turn, it took well over an hour to obtain the necessary letter from a puzzled official. Armed with this and a copy of our contract for irrigation water from the *comunidad de regantes,* in lieu of a letter from the town's water company, we headed for the *ayuntamiento*. They closed for business at two o'clock, but we had half an hour in hand.

The Annoying Little Git had gone home early!

Next morning we arrived at the *ayuntiamento* bright and early, fired up and determined to accept no more nonsense. But when presented with the papers he had specifically requested, the man came up with an unbelievably bizarre tactic. He feigned complete surprise, claiming no knowledge of us or of Isabella.

Alison remonstrated as far as her language capabilities would allow, stressing words like: "many times" - "here" - *"primera ocupación"* - "necessary" - "now".

His reaction was to produce a blank application form, identical to the one we had filled in three months earlier, instructing us to go away and fill it in. He then turned his attention to a file on his desk, indicating that the interview was at an end. We refused to move. I rang Isabella on my mobile to relate this extraordinary turn of events. She was amazed, not to say affronted.

"But this is not possible. What is he thinking? We have been working on this for more than two years now. I went through the papers with the application four days ago. Your file was sitting on his desk. The man is mad. Give him the telephone. Let me talk to him immediately."

I passed it over and we watched as, without comment, he listened to whatever was being said. Finally, muttering something incomprehensible, he switched off the phone and thrust it back at me.

With many sighs, he made a show of searching through the stacks of files on his desk until, apparently to his great surprise, discovered our file sitting on top of one of them. We were kept waiting for some time whilst he riffled through the papers, pretending to read some of them, before shaking his head and declaring that the documents were not sufficient.

Alison said *Qué* rather forcefully, and he repeated that he needed more documents.

Totally out of character, Alison began to shout at the man, her voice beginning to break up with frustration and anger.

"We bring papers. You ask for more. We bring papers. You ask for more. This is mad!"

The ALG merely shrugged, although one could see he was becoming uncomfortable. Everyone else in the office had stopped work, transfixed. Alison continued.

"What do you want? Write on a paper. Everything you want. Write! Now!"

Reluctantly, the man produced a scrap of paper and began to make a list that amounted to fifteen separate items including various reports, applications, authorisations, and letters of confirmation. He handed it across.

"Esta todo?" (Is this everything?)

"Si."

"Nada mas?" (Nothing more?)

"No."

"Sufficiente para la licencia de primera ocupación?"

"Si"

We studied the list. Fortunately, it included most of the letters, contracts and permissions we had already provided. We noticed, however, that the certificate from the water company was still included. Alison pointed at this.

"This is not possible. No house in the country has water from the town. Correct?"

The man looked shifty, but did not react.

"Correct?"

The man still did not react.

173

"You have our contract from the comunidad de regantes. No water from town. Reiga water only. Do you understand?"

His weaseling way out from answering the question was to explain that, unfortunately, it was not within his power to accept or reject documents. These decisions had to be made by the *Técnico.*

"Where is the office of the Técnico? We will ask him now."

"That is not possible. The Técnico does not have the file. It will go to him when I have completed it."

Indicating the heaps of files on his desk, he said that this could take three for four weeks. So saying, he tossed our file dismissively back on to one of the piles, selected someone else's file and started reading as though we were not there.

We were so taken aback by this display of rudeness and incompetence that we just stood there for a few moments and gawped. Then Alison said very loudly and with heavy irony.

"Muchas gracias para su ayuda". (Thank you very much for you help).

If only we had the language...

The next morning, still fuming, we paid a call on Isabella to report this latest farce. They were obviously determined to hold up the *primera ocupación* as long as possible. She listened with concern and made notes. Then she sprang a surprise.

"Ah, but there is good news. When I was at the *ayuntamiento* with your papers a few days ago, we were looking through the old file on the property and I discovered a paper showing that the house was already rated. Mm? There was even a photograph of the old house. I do not know how he (she was referring to the ALG) could have missed it. It was in the file all the time. The house was registered years ago. So the application is not necessary after all. That is good news, yes?"

We were not sure whether to be furious or pleased. Seven wasted months and another expensive and unnecessary trip to Spain. Not to mention the deterioration of one's mental health.

"So the house is now registered in your name. I can check with the *Técnico* that the water contract is not a problem and, if necessary, go with the official to inspect the house again. Once this is done, I will have the *licencia de primera ocupación* notorised, then show it to the *Sevillana.* Mm? Within one or two days they will connect your electricity. Progress at last. Yes?"

CHAPTER TWENTY-EIGHT
Can We Drink The Water?

NOVEMBER 2005 - Wales

An email from Isabella with two pieces of encouraging news. The *Sevillana* had agreed that the electricity could be connected. However, it could not be switched on until they were given a copy of the *licencia de primera ocupación,* which should be issued within the month.

At last. Perhaps, on the next visit to Spain we would be able to move into our house. It had only been five years since we purchased the property.

JANUARY 2006 - Wales

Another message from Isabella. There is a slight hold-up!

"Unfortunately, the people at the *ayuntamiento* have thought up another reason to delay your *primera ocupación.* I do not know why, but they require a *proyecto* (plan) of the sewage system including all the pipework. I am sure that your builder has installed many of these and never been asked for such a thing. However, I have asked Luciana to prepare a drawing. This has to be sent to an office in Malaga for approval."

FEBRUARY 2006 - Wales

A phone call from Isabella about another idiotic demand from the *ayuntamiento.*

"We now have to provide proof that your water is potable. It is a new rule. All new houses must have clean drinking water. This is a joke, mm? *Regantes* water is definitely not drinkable and nobody in the hills has mains water. I will write a strong letter pointing this out. Meanwhile, I have heard that Malaga is not satisfied with Luciana's drawings. They have decided that it is necessary to make an inspection."

It took many weeks to arrange the inspection. No one was available. When a date was finally agreed, the inspector arrived but, seeing the muddy track up the hill (it had been raining), refused to take his car up. Another date was set when Isabella hired a 4x4 vehicle to drive him to the house herself. We were learning that Spanish lawyers are slightly more "hands on" than their British counterparts.

176

Unfortunately, on the appointed day, there had been a lot more rain and the *rio seco* (dry riverbed) was in spate. Another time and another hire of the 4x4 had to be arranged. This all took place over a period of five months and another two months passed before reporting their findings. Their conclusion was that the septic tank, a modern device that processed the sewage to produce pure water, was too near a river and could cause pollution. Isabella had to refute this claim by sending a map and pointing out that the house was way up in the hills and the nearest riverbed was some two miles away down in the valley with houses and a road in between. Moreover, the septic tank performed within EU standards, processing the sewage to produce pure water.

This ridiculous farce went on for eleven months before they finally accepted Isabella's argument. An approval report was delivered to the *ayuntamiento,* who then decided that photos had to be taken of the house before the *licencia de primera ocupación* could be issued. They already had a complete set of photos on file with Luciana's completion documents, but apparently these were not good enough. It had to be their own photographer who, surprisingly, had no space in his diary for quite a while. They managed to put this off until May.

We had no plans for another trip to Spain. Our hostility to the country's bureaucracy had got the better of us once again. It was to be twenty months from our last short trip before we set foot on Spanish soil again. Meanwhile, we got on with our lives. Alison entered a competition for the best play submitted by a writer living in Wales - and won the prize! She was also busy performing her other plays around the country while researching and writing another one. There is a welcome distraction for me when the USITT (United States Institute of Technical Theatre) invited me to a convention in Phoenix Arizona to receive a Distinguished Career in Sound Design Award. This was prompted by the fact that I had recently published my book on the history of sound in the theatre. It just proves that if you write a book everybody takes you seriously and thinks you know what you are talking about.

JUNE 2007 - Spain 10 days
We could not continue to ignore our sad little home in the hills for ever, so eventually we made a short trip, staying once again in Maro. The house was still standing there, patiently waiting for someone to bring it to life.

There was a disconcerting development. On the other side of the valley, a hill had disappeared and bulldozers were flattening more ground. Was this the new motorway? If so, it would be well within our view. But judging from where they were working, a bridge to span the valley would have to be so high it did not seem feasible. We determined to ask our neighbours.

Antonio and Josefina seem pleased to see us, but could not understand why, after all these years, we had not moved in. It was too complicated to explain. We just said: *"ayuntamiento"* and *"mas y mas papeles"* (more and more papers) and they nodded sympathetically. Regarding our concerns about the motorway, they just shrugged their shoulders. No one knew, apparently.

With some trepidation, we paid a call on Isabella. She only ever had bad news and we had not communicated for a while. Sure enough, the enemy had just come up with another good one. We had forgotten that the question of potable water had not been resolved and they were now saying that the house could not be occupied unless a water purification system was installed.

"OK. we will organise it."

We contacted Rafael who talked to his plumber but he had not heard of this regulation. Neither had a local plumbing and heating company. Nobody had any idea of what was required. Isabella put in a phone call to the relevant department at the *ayuntamiento* and demanded more information. They were unable to come up with an answer. When she persisted, they promised to phone back in an hour or two when they had looked up the regulation. They did not phone back, of course, but Isabella put in another call. There was no official answer, but the person she talked to suggested that a chlorine unit would be acceptable.

We approached a local plumbing and heating company called Urena. Gabriel, a helpful young man, had a fair grasp of English that he was eager to practice.

"We have more English customers come to us now. I like to speak. It is good for my business. How can I you help?"

We explained what we needed. He seemed amused.

"No, this is not correct. For a swimming pool, yes. It is not sensible for chlorine water into the house. You cannot drink. Not good. It has smell. The installation is much much money."

"We understand that, but it is necessary or the *ayuntamiento* will not give us our *primera ocupación*."

This he understood. Reluctantly, he prepared an estimate on his computer, printed it out and, with many apologies handed it over. It was going to cost us another £1,200. But if this is what it would take to finally get permission to live in our house, there was no alternative but to ask him to go ahead.

Once again, we were grateful for the speed and efficiency of most private contractors in this part of the world. Within three days, two engineers had built a small brick house beside our *deposito* and routed the water supply to the house through a complicated unit with gauges and timers and pumps. We bought two large bottles of chlorine. These cost 20 euros each and were only expected to last for eight days.

After we had left, Gabriel sent a certificate for the work to the *ayuntamiento* and their engineer inspected and approved the system. We waited to see what idiotic rule they might think up next, hoping that they might have run out of ideas.

But it was the electricity company, the *Sevillana,* who created the next hiatus.

CHAPTER TWENTY-NINE
Too Much Water

After hearing nothing for some four months, an email from Isabella arrived informing us that our electricity could not be connected because the installation was not completed according to the regulations. She had shown them Alphonso's plans along with the *permiso* they had signed, but was told that the rules had changed during the past two years and it did not now comply. She was seeking advice from Alphonso.

NOVEMBER 2007 - Spain for 5 days
A month later, Isabella emailed to say that there had been a breakthrough with the electricity problem. A flying visit was arranged including a hotel in Almuñécar for the three days. It was pouring with rain when we arrived and continued to pour the following day when travelling to Isabella's office in Nerja where she brought us up to date.

"I went to see the electricity people, as I told you, and argued that is was not reasonable to ask us to comply with their new rules retrospectively, but they would not listen. So I managed to persuade Alphonso to attend a meeting at the *Sevillana.*

"When the man insisted that the cable installed under the road to the house was too small a gauge, there was an argument about what they had and had not agreed, but the man could not remember the details. That is, until Alphonso produced a receipt for the bribe the man had accepted. Then the man remembered, mm? Luckily, Alphonso had kept that piece of paper.

"There followed a lot of technical talk I did not understand. But, finally, it was agreed. As soon as we have the *primera ocupación* they will definitely connect your electricity."

That was great, but nothing had been heard from the *ayuntamiento* since the chlorine system had been installed, so Isabella suggested that we should head off in that direction to ask why our *primera ocupación* had not been issued.

Once again, we trouped into the familiar room at the *ayuntamiento* with its depressing atmosphere. Nothing had changed. The ALG, a cigarette hanging from the corner of his mouth, was sitting moodily at his desk, still surrounded by mounds of files. It made one wonder how many other poor people he was torturing.

Isabella began by pointing out that the chlorine installation had been approved by his engineer four months ago. Why had she not heard anything? His explanation was that, regrettably, Urena's completion certificate had to be certified by the *Técnico* and, unfortunately, the job of *Técnico* was currently vacant. Of course, as soon as there was a new *Técnico* and this person had time to certify the document and pass it back to him, the *licencia de primera ocupación* could be prepared. This would only take him two days.

Once back out in the corridor, Isabella was determined to discover when the new man might be appointed and we headed for the office of the *Técnico*. It was just as well we did for what we discovered here was quite unexpected. The woman in the office was completely mystified by our enquiry, insisting that the job of *Técnico* was not vacant and he would not be involved in certifying Urena's certificate anyway. It was the engineer who would be dealing with this matter but as they had recently moved offices, he was still doing paperwork from August last year. We could not speak to him at present as he was not in the building.

Dispirited and angry at being given such a hard time by these petty officials, and even lied to, we asked Isabella if there was not someone higher up who could knock a few heads together? She agreed to try. At the reception desk, she asked if the *Jefe* (Chief) was available, but no appointments were available for several days.

As we parted, Isabella promised to organize a meeting with the *Jefe* as soon as she was back in the office with her diary, and to telephone the engineer repeatedly until she got hold of him.

We needed something to cheer ourselves up before going home, so despite the foul weather we determined to renew our acquaintance with the house we had not seen for five months. In November, it tends to get dark around five o'clock but when we set off in the early afternoon, because of the heavy cloud cover the light was already pretty poor.

Arriving at the *rio seco* we were disconcerted to find it awash with brown muddy water flowing rapidly down from the mountains. Alison wanted us to abandon the excursion but I assured her that the river could only be a few inches deep. Cautiously, I nosed our little hire car forward with the water swirling past our wheels up to the hubs. Alison, tight-lipped, hissed: "This is stupid!" But I was confident we could make it. Suddenly one of the front wheels hit a submerged rock with a metallic crunch and the car came to an abrupt halt, causing Alison to cry out: "Stop! I mean it!" Admitting defeat, I cautiously manoeuvered the vehicle round and headed back to terra firma.

We knew that the locals used another route when the river was impassable so we decided to give it a go. The road started in another part of the town and wound steeply up the other side of the mountain. We did not know what to expect, but although it was narrow and very steep in parts, for most of the way we were driving on a tarmac surface, passing a number of expensive-looking properties. It was raining hard, foggy, and growing darker as we arrived at a fork in the road where the tarmac ran out. The choice was to carry on upwards or head off and down to the right. Certain that we must have climbed higher than our house by now, we opted to turn right. A disastrous decision, as it turned out.

Driving along the narrow track was not a problem at first, but soon it became quite steep and the wheels on one side of the car dropped into a gulley created by the torrent of water rushing down the muddy surface. Fortunately, the vehicle was tilted towards the hillside because, on the outer edge, there was a sheer drop. As the gradient increased, the gulley became deeper and the car began to lean at a more worrying angle. We stopped to review the situation. It was impossible to turn round and reversing up the steep and slippery surface with zero visibility through the rain-lashed rear window was out of the question.

Continuing to edge forward for a short distance, a gap in the hillside appeared with a small flat area leading to someone's *deposito*. If we could back into that, we should be able to turn round. Braving the rain, Alison got out of the car to give directions. She was wearing an anorak, but in seconds her trousers and shoes were completely sodden.

Nervously, I put the gears of the little Fiat hatchback into reverse and gingerly let out the clutch. The wheels began to spin on the muddy slope and the car started to slip sideways towards the abyss, but one of the tyres must have hit rock beneath the slurry because the car jerked backwards and then came to a shuddering halt. One of the back wheels was down in the gulley. Alison tapped on the window and said firmly, "You need to get out now, David."

I knew the car was at an angle, but I was not prepared for the sight of the vehicle with one wheel down to the axle in mud and the opposite front wheel about a foot in the air and inches from a precipice. With the car at this crazy angle, any thoughts of trying to move it were pointless. What to do? Well, whenever, we had a problem we always did the same thing - ring our *abogada*. Isabella was remarkably unfazed by our predicament and said that she would telephone the police. They would come and rescue us. It was their job.

A few minutes later, she rang back with the news that the police were not prepared to venture into the hills because it was too foggy and they might get stuck. Great! What to do now? Isabella's suggestion was to make our way to our neighbours' house.

Not knowing exactly where we were, it seemed sensible to continue the way we had been going, so we set off slithering and slipping down the muddy track. After a few minutes it ended at a junction with a larger track that we recognised as the way up to our house. We had turned off too soon and should have continued driving upwards. It took another ten minutes trudging up the hill in the driving rain to reach our house where there was an umbrella hanging behind the door. We had no water and no electricity but, being British, we did have an umbrella. Equipped with a little more shelter from the rain, we continued up the hill to knock on our neighbours' door. They were somewhat surprised at the sight of this bedraggled pair standing outside their front door and we were quickly invited in and placed in front of a roaring log fire. Josefina made us some welcome coffee while we explained, as best we could, how our car had been abandoned.

Knowing that Antonio would not normally attempt the drive down to town in this kind of weather, we were bracing ourselves for a long walk back to our hotel in Almuñécar. We were, therefore, extremely grateful when, following a short exchange between Josefina and Antonio in which she clearly told him what he had to do, Antonio put on his raincoat and indicated that we should make a dash for his van. It was a perilous journey. The track was fast deteriorating with the rushing water creating even deeper ruts and, in places, washing away the edge of the road altogether. Even though Antonio must have travelled this route hundreds of times, he drove with extreme caution. Fortunately, the van he had bought with the money we had paid him for the house was four-wheel drive. Even so, the wheels slipped alarmingly on several occasions when he braked. Arriving at the hotel, we thanked Antonio effusively and invited him in for a drink, but he was anxious to get back up into the hills before the track became even worse.

Once dried off and with a change of clothes, the next project was to rescue the hire car. There was only one more day available before it had to be returned to the airport. The instructions with the vehicle stated that any problems should be reported to the hire company. This seemed to qualify as a problem, so we put in a telephone call. Once assured that the car had suffered no damage (fingers crossed), they organised a local garage to come to meet us at the hotel the following morning.

The vehicle that turned up was a large flat-bed breakdown truck driven by a small thin grey-haired man in brown overalls. Although the rain had stopped, the ground would still be very muddy, but when we suggested that his vehicle would not be able to negotiate the steep and narrow track, he shrugged off our concerns, indicating that this was all in a day's work for him. So we climbed into the cab and set off.

The riverbed was still awash with water, although considerably less than twelve hours earlier. Lurching through gullies and bumping over rocks beneath the swirling water, we made it to the road that led up into the hills, eventually arriving at the bottom of the track where the Fiat had been abandoned. At this point, our rescuer understood what we had been trying

Floodwater abating in the Rio Seco

to tell him. There was no way he could take his truck up there. Instead, we set off on foot to have a look at the situation. It was a steep climb and our companion was huffing and puffing almost as much as we were by the time we reached the vehicle.

Sizing up the situation, he began collecting stones and packing them into the hole beneath the wheel that was in the air and all around the other tyres. We helped as much as we could, although I saw little point in the exercise.

Then, asking for the keys, he squeezed into the driving seat and fired up the engine. Putting the gears into reverse, he let out the clutch. The back wheels began to spin, but he bounced up and down in the driving seat while putting his foot down on the accelerator. The engine roared, the car shook, the tyres screamed until, suddenly, the car shot backwards. Seemingly out of control it slithered this way and that up the narrow track, several times coming perilously close to the edge. As soon as it came to a halt, he heaved himself out of the vehicle and said in Spanish with a sheepish grin:

"See? No problem."

We expressed our gratitude and admiration of his skill and bravery. Then he said:

"You can drive the car up the track now, yes?"

There was a pause while I contemplated driving backwards up this narrow, slippery, winding track. Noticing the anxious expression on my face, Alison stepped forward and suggested to the man that we would prefer it if he drove the car. He was quite happy to do this, so we followed on foot as he reversed the hundred yards or so up to the junction with the road back to town. Thanking him heartily, we paid the 100 euros he requested for his troubles - money well spent - and he set off to walk back down to his truck.

The following morning at the airport we handed in the car, mightily relieved that apart from a generous splattering of mud, there were no outward signs of what the vehicle had been through.

CHAPTER THIRTY
The Undercover Electrician

JANUARY 2008 - Spain for 6 days

Once more, we were staying in our friends' house in Maro, but we had high hopes that this really would be the last time. Isabella had indicated that the *ayuntamiento* seemed to have run out of ideas for not granting the vital *licencia de primera ocupación* and she was hopeful that it could now be resolved.

The first thing we did was visit Antonio and Josefina to thank them for rescuing us from the rain on our last visit. We had bought some Scottish shortbread in a tin that was shaped like a van similar to theirs, thinking that this would make an amusing gift. We pointed out the figure driving the van and said it was Antonio. They looked puzzled, but thanked us for the present anyhow and invited us in for coffee. The shortbread, not something we had ever seen in Spain, were sampled and generally agreed to be very tasty. It was all very relaxed and they did not seem to mind that we could not hold a proper conversation.

Our fears about the impending motorway were confirmed. An army of men and machines were now constructing impossibly high concrete pillars to carry the road across the valley to a tunnel being gouged out of the hillside. Fortunately, the sound of the machinery at that distance was not too invasive, giving us hope that the traffic noise on the completed motorway would not completely ruin the tranquility we so much enjoyed.

Great news! Isabella telephoned to say that the *notorio* had signed the *licencia de primera ocupación* and it had been delivered to the *ayuntamiento* the day before. So, the following morning, we rushed to collect it. There was no way the ALG could wriggle out of this one. Or was there?

True to form, he was not to give up so easily. Determined to make a last ditch stand, he denied having the document and insisted that he had no idea when it would arrive. Fortunately, on this occasion, we were accompanied by an English-speaking woman, Maria, recently employed by the *ayuntamiento* to assist foreigners like us. We explained to Maria that our *abogada* had been informed by the *notorio* himself that the document was definitely here.

Maria translated this information, whereupon the horrible little man made a great show of looking through all the files on his desk. Apparently drawing a blank, he picked up his telephone and made a call. He was a poor actor and we strongly suspected that he was not actually talking to anyone. Replacing the receiver, he announced that it would arrive in half an hour.

So, it was off for coffee.

Upon our return, our delightful friend handed over the precious document without managing to look at us. After waiting all this time - eight long years - it was a bit of a let down; just a single sheet of paper with two large date stamps, each signed by the *notorio,* over a little bit of typing. Still, it was definitely headed *licencia de primera ocupación* so, presumably, that was it. Being properly brought up, we said "gracias" to the horrid little man - who did not reply - and left, hoping never to see his weasel face ever again.

We had waited so long that it took a while to sink in. Nobody could now stop us from moving into our house. Pausing only to make copies of the *licencia* at the photocopy shop, we presented ourselves at the office of the *Sevillana*. The electricity would be switched on in two days time - first thing in the morning!

Following a celebratory lunch at a splendid fish restaurant in Almuñécar, we felt the need to talk to our builder. We had water, so long as Antonio was happy to continue filling our *deposito,* so all that was needed to make the place a going concern was some gas for the water heater. Rafael had previously scorned the idea of waiting for some official to come and fit the gas bottles, saying they were always available if you knew where to get them. Taking him at his word, we called him on his mobile and the following morning he arrived, produced two bottles from his van and connected them to the heater. Apart from reimbursing him for the cost, that was all there was to it. Apparently, when a bottle became empty, we could swap it for a full one at the local petrol station and nobody would ask questions. The source of these bottles was not explained and we did not enquire.

On the morning when the electricity was supposed to be switched on, we drove up to our property, trying not to get too excited in case there had been a hitch. Entering the house with some trepidation, I turned on the kitchen light. Nothing. Typical. Then I remembered the fuse box. Sure enough, the main contactor was in the "off" position. I switched it on and - wow - the electricity had been connected. We turned on the lights in other rooms and they all worked. Lights everywhere! Fantastic! This called for a celebration. Having had the foresight to bring bottled water and milk, we could actually make our first cup of tea. Alison switched on the kettle and all the fuses tripped out.

I put them back on and they tripped out again. After a few experiments, it became clear that we could have either the kettle, the oven, or the lighting switched on, but not any two at the same time. I could only think that this was something to do with the compromise solution agreed by Alphonso and the man at the *Sevillana*. Because the supply cable was deemed to be too small, they had installed a similarly small master fuse. As the fuse was in a sealed unit, this could not be verified.

I phoned Isabella who said there was no point in contacting Alphonso. He had supplied us with electricity, been paid and wanted nothing more to do with us. However, she knew an electrician in Nerja who spoke a little English and would ask him to come and have a look. A little while later she phoned back to say that he would be with us at ten o'clock the following morning.

Dead on time, a tall young man in blue overalls pulled up at the house, slightly put out because that he had just driven his smart new car along a riverbed and up a very rough track. He explained in his pretty good English:

"This car was designed for driving on flat roads in the town, not for riverbeds and mountains. But never mind, I am here now, so where are your fuses?"

Following some tests, he confirmed that the company fuse was only 10 amps.

"This is no good. You cannot run a house on 10 amps, but I see why they do this. The cable from the meter on the pylon to your fuse box is very long. The cable should be bigger, so they put in a small fuse. That way, they stop you to use much electricity."

"But the cables on poles you see everywhere all around the hills are no bigger than ours. They provide electricity to thousands of houses."

"For many years, yes. This is correct. No problem. But now there is new rule. The Sevillana will not agree. It is necessary to have a bigger cable. I can do this for you with money more or less 4,000 euros."

We were stunned at this bombshell and when Alison explained we had paid the equivalent of £14,000 for the installation only two years previously with documentation and written permission from the *Sevillana,* he was appalled.

He considered the situation for a while before taking me by the arm and leading me out of the front door into the garden. What he was going to say was man's talk. Not for the delicate ears of the little woman. He spoke in a low conspiratorial voice and I had to move in close to hear:

"I could do this another way."

"Go on."

"There is an illegal solution."

"I like the sound of this."

"What I can do - and this is not legal - is remove the company's master fuse."

"I thought the main fuse was necessary to make it all work."

"Not necessary. I take it away. No problem."

"But is this safe?"

"Yes, is safe because every circuit in the house has fuse automatic."

"A trip fuse."

"Yes. Trip fuse. So if there is a fault anywhere, the automatic fuse will trip. No problem. I can do this for you with money 40 euros."

"Wonderful. Fantastic. Please do it."

"The only thing is nobody must know who did this."

"Of course not."

"Is important. This could be trouble for me."

"I understand. Nothing will ever be said"

"You must never say my name."

I insisted that I did not know who he was and, if anybody should ever ask about the fuses, I would deny all knowledge. Solemnly, we shook hands.

Back in the house, it took him less than five minutes to perform the deed. Then, lo and behold, unlimited amounts of electricity were suddenly unleashed. We had lights, the cooker, fridge and freezer were all working, and wonderful water came pouring from our taps when, for the first time, the pump in our *deposito* sprang into life. We were ecstatic. Alison put on the kettle, but our saviour nervously refused our offer of tea or coffee. Although pleased, and not a little surprised, to see his clients so pathetically grateful for his endeavours, he could not wait to leave the scene of the crime. Bidding a hasty "Adios", he headed back to town.

Now that the house had electricity, water and gas, we were in business. Unfortunately, there was only one more day before we had to leave for England, but what the hell. Furniture, bedding, towels and all the basics required for living had already been unpacked from their eight-year sojourn in the wine store, so we checked out of the hotel, purchased a few provisions, and MOVED IN.

CHAPTER THIRTY-ONE
El Escondrijo

MARCH 2008 - Spain for 21 days

For the first time since we had purchased the property just over eight years ago, we were actually going to be living in our house. Alison had refused bookings for her shows for the next three weeks. For my part, I was determinedly retired - although I seemed to remain busy doing something or other. With no major crisis looming - hopefully - we looked forward to twenty-one restful days in the sunshine.

The motorway now stretched most of the way across the valley, but all work seemed to have ceased. The reason for this silence was explained when next we spoke to Isabella. There had been a major disaster when a section of the roadway under construction had collapsed and seven workmen had fallen hundreds of feet to their deaths. This tragedy was now the subject of an investigation and insurance claims and it would be many months before work could resume.

Apart from the motorway, our view had changed a good deal over the years. It was still spectacular, but more than double the number of little country houses had sprung up along the valley and on the hills opposite. How they had all obtained permission was a complete mystery to us.

Having given so much thought to the layout of the house, it all worked perfectly. The feeling of space in such a small building was a constant marvel. The only thing I appeared to have got wrong was the height of the kitchen surfaces. I had allowed too much space above the height of a fridge, not knowing how thick the cement structure was going to be, and had forgotten to discuss this with Rafael. The height I had given for the surfaces was a metre when it should have been 92 centimetres (three feet). For me, with a dodgy back, this was a good working height but for Alison, not being very tall, found it a problem particularly when cutting up vegetables or working at the sink.

She tried buying some very thick platform shoes and the sight of a taller Alison tottering around the kitchen in enormous bright pink footwear was quite startling. Back in England, we bought a flat-pack from Ikea and on our next visit I gave it an "old Spanish kitchen" make-over. The sides were clad in ply and the melamine drawer fronts  were replaced with timber, all stained dark walnut, as was the wooden edging on the top framing some colourful patterned tiles. Job done. With a work surface of the right height, the pink shoes were abandoned.

The house had no proper address, just the number of our parcel of land in an area locally known as *La Renta*, so we thought it should be given a name. Located high up in the hills on an unnamed dirt road accessed from a dry riverbed, it is very difficult to find if you are not well acquainted with the area. We find this remoteness and inaccessibility rather appealing and when trying to think of a name for our little cottage we looked up the Spanish word for "Hiding Place" or "Hideout". It turned out to be *El Escondrijo.* This sounded good enough for us. So *El Escondrijo* (pronouced "escond<u>ee</u>ho") it became.

With the electricity working, the underfloor heating could be connected. The daytime temperature was usually quite hot in March, but the evenings were sometimes a little chilly; in which case, the house could be pleasantly warmed with the tiled floors heated just enough to walk around in stocking feet.

Urena came to test the system for providing "clean" water and declared that everything was working perfectly. Concerned at the costs of paying 20e for a chlorine bottle every eight days for the privilege of having the water in the house smelling like a swimming pool, we paid a call on our friend Roger and asked his opinion.

"You must be joking! Do you realise what the chlorine is doing to your septic tank? Only killing off all the micro-organisms that keep it working. That's all. Do you really want to live with the smell of chlorine inside the house and the smell of sewage outside the house? I don't care what the *ayuntamiento* says. The whole idea is bollocks."

Taking note of his considered advice, we switched off the whole system and there it stood, doing nothing, ever several years. Eventually, it was dismantled altogether when we needed the little brick house it occupied for something else.

Once again, we admired Roger's lush garden and as our parched plot of land received no water for most of the year, assumed that we could never aspire to anything like this. However, Roger pointed out several succulents and even a couple of trees that could survive without water. We were given an assortment of cacti that he happened to be throwing out and Pepe was dispatched to cut a piece off a strange kind of succulent-cum-tree. The piece he presented to us was just a stick about eighteen inches long with no growth and no roots. The instruction was to stick it in the ground and leave it. This we did, with no confidence that it would survive, yet alone grow into a large tree. Five years on it was to become more than eight feet (2.5m) high with four branches spreading out so wide that two of them had to be cut off.

Some of the little cacti also grew to be so enormous that they eventually ran out of space and sadly, because they are such wonderful creations, had to be cut down and dug up. No mean task. Once taken root, they were determined to stay put.

During our final week, bravely, we invited Antonio and Josefina for an English tea with egg sandwiches (we could not find a cucumber anywhere) and a cake that Alison baked that morning. We wondered how long we could keep a conversation going, but they stayed for two hours, putting up with Alison's faltering attempt at small talk plus a couple of sentences from me that I had previously worked out and written down. We think they are probably amused and slightly mystified by us.

In conversation, the subject of water inevitably came up. Antonio was still running a hose down the hill every time we needed water and we reintroduced the idea of Rafael installing some permanent pipework. For some reason we did not understand, Rafael had not installed this some months ago as requested and we wondered whether there might have been some clash of personalities between him and Antonio. The situation became clear when Antonio explained that he was not happy to have a trench dug across his land where he was growing crops. However, he had an alternative plan. Unfortunately, we could not follow what he was saying and, seeing our confusion, beckoned us to follow him out of the house and down to the bottom of our land. Here, beside the rough road, he lifted a large metal cover to reveal a concrete chamber. Inside were two large stopcocks connected to the *regantes* water system. One of these used to supply water to his land before he built his big new water tank. He still had the right to use this stopcock and as joint owners of the land, so did we.

Having a separate water supply from the *comunidad de regantes* would be ideal, although we would have to build a larger *deposito*. This was great news. We only wished that it had been mentioned before.

A visit to the *regantes* office confirmed that a connection to a larger tank would not be a problem, although they did suggest that a *licencia de obras* from the inevitable *ayuntamiento* would be required.

Oh, no. Not the Annoying Little Git again!

We were assured us that this would be a formality as water is vital in the *campo* and *depositos* are being built all the time.

Back at the house, I found a plan of our land on the computer and printed a copy showing a new 60,000 litre tank sitting alongside our existing 10,000 litre tank. Connected together, they would hold sufficient water for irrigating our garden and some of the olive and fruit trees that were looking a little sad following several years without water.

Then, here we were, back at the *ayuntamiento* once more. Thank goodness Maria, the English interpreter, was there to smooth the way when we presented the plan. True to form, our weasely friend was his usual uncommunicative self. Following a cursory glance at the drawing, he produced an application form and pushed it across the desk. Knowing the drill, we filled in our details, signed it and handed it back. He then marked it with a large date stamp, clipped it to the drawing and, mumbling something to Maria, tossed it onto a pile of papers. Maria translated that we would receive the *permiso* in two to three weeks. Well, yes. How many times had we heard that before?

Nevertheless, we were totally relaxed. However long it took, it would not affect the lifestyle we were now able to enjoy. Already, memories of the disappointments and frustrations of the previous years were beginning to fade. It was hard to believe how, at our lowest point, we had contemplated selling up and never visiting Spain again.

So ended the first blissful month living in *El Escondrijo*.

EL ESCONDRIJO – 2008

197

CHAPTER THIRTY-TWO
Driving Down Spain

We have a little Yorkshire Terrier called Burton - after Richard Burton, of course, as the dog was born in South Wales - who stayed with a charming elderly couple while we were away for short periods. But as we now intended to spend weeks rather than days in Spain, this important member of the family had to come with us. As it is not possible to fly with an animal unless caged in a box and shoved in the hold, all journeys in future would have to be made by ferry and car. Consequently, Burtie (as he is known) was chipped, given all the necessary injections, and became the proud possessor of his very own passport.

During the first eighteen-hour voyage on the car ferry to Northern Spain from Plymouth, Burtie was surprised to find himself in a cabin full of kennels containing an assortment of dogs. He endured this indignity quietly, while indicating that it was not appreciated. Dog owners were allowed to visit at any time for some exercise on the wind-blown upper deck, interludes that Burtie viewed as adding insult to injury.

After docking at the port of Santander, the drive down Spain via Madrid and Granada was around eleven and a half hours without stops. But as the ferry did not arrive until early in the afternoon, we decided to drive for only four hours and then rest up at a hotel. Another overnight stay south of Madrid made the last leg of the journey short enough to allow time for food shopping and opening up the house in daylight. We had invested in a four-wheel drive Volvo to cope with the riverbed and the rough mountain tracks and this solid vehicle made the daily trips into Almuñécar feel safer and much more comfortable.

When it became time to return to England, Burtie had to be taken to the vet for a worm pill, medication for ticks, and a general check-up. Being allowed to bring dogs into the UK without spending time in quarantine was fairly recent, and the rules were strict in the early days. A vet had to stamp his passport between twenty-four and forty-eight hours before the boat departed for England, or he would not be allowed to travel; but as the drive up north to the ferry port took more than forty-eight hours, this was tricky.

Rabies had been eradicated in Spain and dogs were free to travel to other European countries, so the vet in Almuñécar considered these British rules to be nonsense. After a cursory examination to make sure that Burtie had all his moving parts, he administered the required medication, then enquired when the ferry departed. Working back forty-eight hours, he filled in the passport with an appropriate time and date. By 2012, the rules had been changed to allow more time between visiting the vet and boarding the ferry and the dog was only required to have a worm pill.

Incredibly, by 2013, the journey from Almuñecar to Santander had been reduced to a little over eight hours. Now entirely motorway, the road was improved by simply bulldozing hills, tunneling through mountains and crossing ravines on roads perched on worryingly high concrete pillars. The capital city of Madrid with its complicated road network was always a nightmare to negotiate, especially during rush hours, but this could now be bypassed by a toll motorway. It cost more than twenty euros to travel around Madrid, but we felt it money well spent.

With the dog Burtie, frequently stops were necessary and we often asked our "Satnav" to find points of interest along the way. One of the suggestions was something called "Pedraza". It did not say what this was and from previous experience it could have been an ancient monument, Roman remains, or even a cheese factory. What we were not expecting was a fabulously picturesque medieval walled town.

Alison and Burtie in Pedraza

Declared a national monument in 1951, the houses have been restored and with no modern buildings the whole place feels like walking through history.

On another occasion, our 'satnav' directed us to *La Cueva de los Enebralejos*, prehistoric caves containing rock carvings and paintings from around 2500 BC with even earlier traces of habitation.

A school party had just completed a tour and were returning to their bus and, being around one o' clock in the afternoon, the staff in the entrance area and shop appeared to be packing up for the day. Nevertheless, we asked a pleasant looking young man, who turned out to be the manager, if it was possible to buy tickets. Officially we were too late, but he offered us a guided tour if we were willing to put up with his poor English. Surprisingly, Burtie was included. This was most unusual as north of Madrid, rather like in England, dogs are seldom tolerated in shops, cafes, or other public areas. As soon as one travels south of Madrid however, the people are much more relaxed about pets and they are normally welcome anywhere. In general, we find the people in the south more relaxed about everything. It must be the sunshine.

There ensued a fascinating three quarters of an hour exploring the underground caverns. Our enthusiastic guide was a keen geologist who, because we were showing genuine interest, took us into "dangerous places" where the public was not allowed. In return, we added to his English vocabulary where we could.

Although these caverns were well worth a visit, they can hardly compare with the gigantic underground Caves of Nerja on the south coast not far from Almuñécar. This series of enormously high caverns with spectacular stalactites and stalagmites stretch for almost three miles, although the public has access to only some of them. Rediscovered in 1959, skeletal remains indicate that the caves were inhabited as far back as around 25,000 BC. In February 2012, it was announced that Neanderthal cave paintings had been discovered that were possibly the oldest yet found in the world. In one of the caverns, concerts and ballet performances are staged during the summer months.

On subsequent journeys up and down the country, we were able to explore a number of the many ruined mediaeval castles one sees perched on top of hills or rocky outcrops. Clambering up to these edifices, many of which had helpful signs and information for tourists, was exhausting during the heat of the day but, however small and remote the local village, there was always a bar or restaurant serving drinks and excellent food.

One of the best hotels we experienced was in Toledo, an hour or so south-west of Madrid.

The hotel Cardenal is an 18th century palace built into the 9th century walls of the old town. Originally the home of Cardinal Lorenzana, it has a lovely walled garden where one can eat or drink in the shade of the trees. At our first meal there, we were surprised to see marzipan listed on the menu as a dessert, not knowing that Toledo is renowned for this confection. It had to be sampled. Three little shapes of marzipan presented on a plate. Delicious!

We explored the city's steep and narrow cobbled streets (that sometimes lead nowhere), climbing right up to the huge Gothic cathedral at its centre, built on the site of a former Grand Mosque. Unfortunately, our exploration lasted a great deal longer than was comfortable when we became hopelessly lost in the maze of streets and alleyways.

On another trip we stayed in a small town some 125 miles south of Madrid called Almagro, one of the many seemingly isolated settlements on the vast flat plain of central Spain. We were not expecting anything of particular interest except for a recommended boutique hotel, so when wandering around the fairly insignificant town square we were astonished to stumble upon the oldest theatre in Spain. Open to the public, it simply had to be investigated.

The *Corral de Comedias* dates back to 1628 and is the only functioning original courtyard theatre in the world. Rediscovered in 1953 during the renovation of the square, the theatre is now celebrated with the annual International Classic Theatre Festival. For a month every year this small town comes alive with performances in the *Corral de Comedias* and other venues including the Municipal Theatre and La Veleta Theatre.

Not only does this little town have three theatres but it is also the location for Spain's National Theatre Museum. This houses a large and impressive collection of costumes, scene designs, models of theatres, photographs of actors and productions going back to 1870, plus over 2,000 items of clothing since the 18th century.

I was particularly pleased to see a number of original mechanical sound effects machines that you are allowed to activate - unlike the few pathetic examples that were in London's Theatre Museum. This uninspiring museum in Covent Garden closed in 2007 and some of the artifacts are now on display in the Victoria and Albert Museum in Kensington. While researching my book on theatre sound, I discovered that the V&A had a collection of wonderful old noise making machines in one of their vast stores. These are never seen - or heard - by the public. In Britain, we pride ourselves on our theatrical heritage, but the modern purpose-built museum in Almalgro celebrating Spain's theatrical history puts us completely to shame.

About three hours drive south of Madrid, La Venta de Gárdenas is a good stopping place. Here we can give Burtie a little exercise in a pleasant wooded area by a river, part of an enormous national park famous for hiking, horse riding and hunting. Nearby is an extraordinary restaurant called Casa Pepe. Dedicated to the memory of the dictator General Franco whose Nationalist forces overthrew the government in 1939 after a very bloody civil war, the outside of the building is painted in the bright yellow and red of the Nationalist flag. Inside, the walls of the very long bar are covered with posters and photographs of *El Generalissimo*. Everywhere there are military hats, medals, banners and other memorabilia of the Spanish civil war and the souvenir shop sells everything from key rings to bottles of wine with the nationalist insignia. It is all a bit spooky but the staff, all male and wearing black T-shirts, serve very good food.

We often listened to story CDs while travelling and one of these was a recording of Richard E. Grant narrating the story of the making of a film he directed in Swaziland called "Wah-Wah". It is a harrowing tale of filming in Africa with a limited budget and a tight schedule, frustrated by an absent French producer who failed to send the promised funds on time for setting up the various locations and paying the cast and crew. Having both experienced similar situations with under-funded theatre productions, we became totally involved in Richard E. Grant's nightmare, genuinely concerned that it was going to end in disaster. We were only brought back to reality when the Volvo gently slowed down and stopped.

I had noted that the tank had enough diesel for at least a hundred miles when we set off but, unaware of time passing, we had been driving at speed for more than two hours. Fortunately, we ran out of fuel near a motorway junction and there was just enough momentum to steer the car on to the hard shoulder.

There were no buildings in sight, but the slip road led up to a flyover and we hoped that there might be some sign of life on the road above. It was midday and extremely hot, but Alison volunteered to investigate as she could make herself understood. I would remain with the car in case the *policia* turned up.

I watched her trudge up the slip road to the flyover where she disappeared from my view. There was then a long wait. On the other side of the motorway, about ten minutes walk from the intersection, Alison was mightily relieved to see a petrol station. Here she was able to buy a can of diesel, but when she made to cross the motorway and head back, the garage man rushed out to stop her. How could the *senora* think of crossing such a dangerous road?

He explained the situation to a young man filling his car at one of the pumps and asked if he could give Alison a lift back to the car. He willingly agreed, although it meant travelling up the motorway for a couple of miles to an intersection in order to turn back onto our carriageway.

On the journey, he explained that he was a teacher of English who had been laid off because of the terrible economic situation in Spain. This was at the height of the recession in 2012. Currently he was still giving lessons at the school for free, although he did not know how much longer this could continue. The country was in a bad shape but the children still needed to learn.

The precious diesel was delivered and when we expressed our gratitude, he replied that he was pleased to have this unexpected opportunity of practicing his English. With that, this kind fellow went on his way.

CHAPTER THIRTY-THREE
Easter

APRIL 2008 - Spain for four weeks

It was Easter and soon after our arrival we presented our neighbours with two Thorntons Easter chocolate bunnies each inscribed with their names in icing. As usual, our gifts were received with pleasure tinged with bafflement. Coffee was produced and Josefina had made some special Easter *empanadas* (fried envelopes of pastry filled with egg, olives, onion and all kinds of herbs). Many were consumed.

Easter is a major event in this Catholic country and we were fascinated to see some of the spectacular processions that take place in the streets during *Semana Santa* (the week leading up to Easter Sunday).

Almuñecar is not a large town, but each day during the week, enormous floats, or platforms, with painted wooden sculptures depicting scenes from the Passion emerge from the main church and are carried through the streets for many hours until finally returning to the church. The people carrying these enormously heavy platforms, and some others in the procession, wear penitential robes with conical shaped hoods (exactly like the Klu Klux Klan). These pointed hoods symbolize a rising towards heaven and also hide the identities of the penitants as they mourn the pain and suffering of Christ. Different coloured robes are worn by a various religious associations, called brotherhoods, who care for the images of Jesus, Mary and the Saints throughout the year while planning the next *Semana Santa* event.

Penitants, including children, lead and follow the floats, walking slowly in time to bands playing loud music, all in a minor key until the Sunday when Christ is risen. Some of the floats are enormously heavy (we counted more than a hundred men labouring under one of these) and can only be carried for short distances. Every thirty or forty metres, a man walking in front of the float rings a bell, the band stops playing and the floats are gently lowered to the ground to give aching limbs a rest. Traditionally, carrying these heavy platforms was an all male affair , but now young girls and women join in and, in Almuñécar, one of the smaller floats is carried entirely by women.

For the parades on Easter Sunday, the penitents remove their hoods in jubilation at the Lord's resurrection. There is also a special ceremony in front of the *ayuntamiento* when three of the huge statues are brought into the crowded square and two figures "come alive" by bending their heads in front of the Jesus figure, which raises a hand in benediction - to tumultuous applause.

The processions taking place in towns all over Spain during *Semana Santa* are incredibly moving and not to be missed. Burtie, on the other hand, did not enjoy the Easter festivities - far too noisy - preferring to remain in the safety and familiar surroundings of the Volvo.

By the time the holiday period was over and everything back to normal, we felt relaxed enough to face the ALG and check on the progress of our *licencia de obras* for the new *deposito*. The ALG was pleased to be able to report that he did not have it. Unfortunately, the engineer had to approve the plan and, sadly, he had not yet done so. It would possibly be resolved in two or three weeks. Not prepared to accept this excuse, we went in search of the engineer's office where we were informed that the engineer did not have our plan and, in any case, could not approve anything without a proper *proyecto*. So that was a waste of two months.

We now had to visit our architect, Luciana, to obtain a *proyecto*. When asked to prepare a design for a round concrete water tank, something farmers have been knocking up all over the countryside for years, she was both surprised and amused. But she was even more surprised when we went on to outline a plan we had been mulling over for creating a guest bedroom in the brick-built store beside the house - hitherto Antonio's wine store and chicken shed. The thought being that we might as well apply for permission for both projects at the same time.

Luciana was highly sceptical about this idea. Certainly, we could not apply for a *reforma* as the building was not constructed to a high enough standard. It would therefore have to be a completely new building and under no circumstances could it be called a living space. She would be willing to do a *proyecto* for an upgraded *trastero* (storeroom) on the understanding that it was extremely unlikely to be accepted.

There was nothing to lose, apart from Luciana's fee, so I set about measuring up and preparing a drawing. The space on the upper level - just big enough for 'storing' a single bed - would have large windows providing plenty of light. To one side, a few steps led down to an intermediate level where there happened to be just space enough for the 'storage' of a shower, WC and washbasin. None of these were marked on the drawing, of course. Below this, the chicken house accessed from the lower terrace would become a further "store" with a window. All floors would be tiled because of the nature of what we intended to store.

The plans were presented to Luciana who, having studied them, gave me an old fashioned look but did not comment. It would take her up to two weeks to turn my ideas into construction drawings and take them along to the *ayuntamiento*. The *deposito* should not be a problem, but would we get away with her application for building the *trastero*? All we could do was wait and see.

CHAPTER THIRTY-FOUR
Francisco

2008 OCTOBER - Spain for four weeks

The *permisos* for the new *deposito* and *trastero* were still not ready, but being well into the "mañana" lifestyle by now, we simply turned our attention to important tasks such as buying hand-painted tiles for our window sills and applying Danish Oil to add a gloss to the dark stained woodwork.

After a week, Luciana had informed us that the *permiso* for the new *deposito* must have been processed by now, so we dropped into the *ayuntamiento* to collect it. Expecting the ALG to have come up with some new ploy to frustrate us, we were not disappointed. Even for him, this was a good one. Fabricating a look of genuine concern and, for once, looking us in the eye, he regretted that he had no memory of ever receiving our application for a *permiso.*

Fortunately, another man who we had not seen before was working at a nearby desk. Saying something to the ALG, he got up, went to one of the filing cabinets and after searching for a while produced our application. The ALG did not look best pleased when the man confirmed that it had been filed back in March and, apologising for the delay, assured us that the paperwork would be completed by the end of the week.

Knowing their sense of time, we actually waited for ten days. To say we were dumfounded at what happened on our return would be putting it mildly. The ALG produced not only a *permiso* for the *deposito*, but a *permiso* for the *trastero* as well. They were actually going to let us build our posh storerooms. As we took our leave, the new man at the nearby desk looked up and gave us a broad smile.

As Rafael was to be on site building the *trastero,* we asked if he could also create some terraces on the other side of the house where it was currently just a steep incline covered in weeds. This was agreed and the plan was to start demolishing the old store in the New Year and complete all the work by the following August. Unfortunately, as he had become very busy during the months waiting for permission to build, he could not undertake the *deposito* as well. This left us with the problem of finding another builder.

The thought of pouring more money into *El Escondrijo* was a little worrying as the paperwork was still not complete. We had never received the official registration of our house and now the Registry Office had told Isabella the reason for this long hold-up. They were concerned that the second house on the jointly owned land, that being ours, had been built as a commercial venture. They wanted us to sign a document guaranteeing that our house had been built to live in not to sell.

As the joint ownership arrangement meant that any legal documents pertaining to either property had to be approved by the four of us, we all had to troupe down to the Registry Office once again with Isabella to sign yet another piece of paper. Half an hour later, we were still hanging around outside the office and although this must have been the fourth or fifth occasion our neighbours had been asked to go through this tedious process, they never complained.

While filling in the time chatting to Isabella, we queried how Antonio had managed to build his house without us signing any documents. On the contrary, Isabella explained, we did actually sign a building application with our previous *abogado,* Waltravens. At that time, we were dealing with so many documents, not to mention language problems, that this one must have slipped through. The fact that Waltravens got us to sign this agreement was, of course, the start of all our problems.

As the minutes ticked by, the subject of builders and *depositos* came up and Antonio suggested that one of his cousins, Francisco Martin Martin, might possibly be our man. Of course, we jumped at the idea, so he put in a call on his mobile and it was arranged that his cousin would drop by that evening.

Our introduction to Francisco was typical of the man. Alerted to someone shouting *"Hola! Hola!"*, we rushed to the front door to find a man in baggy grey trousers and a shirt that looked a size to large, standing the other side of the front gate gesticulating to be let in. It was not locked and he could easily have pushed it open. Upon realising this, he laughed uproariously. Life for him, we were to learn, was a series of miscomprehensions and misunderstandings, the discovery of which were always greeted with wide-eyed surprise followed by peels of laughter.

Recovering, he introduced himself and proffered a large hand, which Alison and I duly shook.

Entering the house, I showed him Luciana's drawing. He squinted at this for some time, muttering to himself, with a puzzled expression. Then, rather worryingly, he asked what size we would like the *deposito.* When I pointed out that all the measurements were clearly shown on the drawing, he made a helpless gesture and admitted that he had forgotten to bring his *gafas* (glasses) without which everything was a blur. The thought of his stupidity brought on another bout of laughter. There followed an awkward pause before Alison had the idea of proffering her own glasses. They were far too small for his large face and although the side pieces did not reach his ears, he managed to balance them precariously on his bulbous nose. This caused more merriment. Turning to peer at the drawing, he exclaimed:

"Perfect! A miracle! I can see everything. Much better than my own glasses. Look, the size of the deposito is on the drawing. See?"

More laughter ensued, but it soon became clear that something was worrying him. He had successfully built *depositos* for other people without drawings and without *permisos* and knew how to cost them; but this one, designed by an architect, required massive foundations, thicker walls and an unbelievable amount of iron reinforcement. If we really wanted him to build such a thing, he would have to go away and work out a price.

Upon his return the following evening, Antonio heard the car draw up and joined us to discuss the problems of constructing the big round tank on our steeply sloping site. Francisco had the estimate but had forgotten his glasses again. We began to wonder if he did actually own any. Alison's *gafas* were called upon once again. As the two men discussed the over-specification of what to them should have been a simple structure, there was a great deal of head shaking. Accepting the inevitable, they began pacing the land with Francisco enthusiastically explaining how he intended to proceed. Antonio, an experienced builder, interrupted several times with alternative suggestions causing Francisco to pause, a worried frown on his face. Then, having grasped the concept, he always eagerly agreed that this was the best way to do it.

Finally, the two men declared themselves happy and we arranged to pay Francisco fifty percent of his estimate. In the Spanish way, the total price for tax purposes was far less than the actual cost, which was a whacking 14,000 euros. This we considered worth paying if it meant that we were no longer reliant on other people for our water. Our real concern that the project was in the hands of this likeable but muddle-headed man was allayed when Antonio confided that he would be overseeing the work.

During our final week, we caught up with Rafael to confirm a few details on what he would be doing for us, and we noticed that he was not his usual cheery self. We were aware that he had been building a house in Maro, expecting to sell it at a good profit. Unfortunately, during the year or so since he had started to build, the financial crisis that started in America and quickly spread to Europe had hit Spain badly. His timing could not have been worse. The boom that had seen houses, hotels and blocks of flats springing up all along the coast for the past few years suddenly came abruptly to an end. Property prices fell by around 50% almost overnight. Everywhere one could see the skeletons of abandoned building projects and motionless cranes left by bankrupt construction companies.

Although not completed, Rafael was desperate to find a buyer in order to free himself of a crippling bank loan. He asked if we knew anyone who might wish to buy. Unfortunately, we did not. Our only suggestion was to publicise the property at local hotels catering for foreigners, most of whom were English speakers. To this end, I took photographs of his house and prepared a sales leaflet on my computer for him to distribute. Sadly, there were no takers and seven years later he had still not found a buyer.

2009 MAY- Spain for five weeks

Francisco had completed the *deposito,* an impressive construction supported at the front by a high stone down wall to the terrace below. The wall was a metre out from the *deposito* to create a walkway providing easy access to the pump house; an important addition to the design instigated by Antonio.

We still had to purchase water from Antonio as Francisco had yet to install a pipe to the *regantes* stopcock at the bottom of our land. Currently, he was off doing a job for someone else, so we would just have to wait.

Alison could now communicate with her clients in England at an internet shop in Almuñécar, so it was not a problem being away from the UK. Determined to have no dealings with *abogadas*, planning offices or *ayuntamientos,* this turned out to be a blissful interlude at *El Escondrijo.*

*

JUNE 2009 – Wales

Inspired by living in *El Escondrijo* where, although pint-sized, everything was exactly how we liked it, I was keen to see if we could design a house that similarly suited our needs in England; so we put Tal-y-Fan Farm on the market and bought a plot of land with a tumbledown cottage in the Forest of Dean with permission to demolish the cottage and build a new house. We must have been mad!

My initial plans for an L-shaped cottage style building with interesting windows and gables were rejected out of hand by the planning department. Roofs at different heights and anything not "lined up" was against the rules, as was anything built in brick. "Whose rules?" we wondered. Other buildings in the area varied from old cottages and farmhouses to a couple of recently built "executive homes". We pointed out that there was a modern red brick bungalow within sight of our plot that must have been built during the past ten years, but were informed that the rules had changed. Where had we heard that before? Although the plot was bordered by farmland on three sides, they wanted a square two-story town house with a central front door and identically sized windows all in line horizontally and vertically.

Planners!

Fortunately, everyone spoke English this time and following the submission of several sketches, a design was approved. The compromise was a bungalow with the boring frontage they wanted - but we were allowed to let rip at the back. Facing south and onto the garden with fields beyond, all the main living space was on this side of the house with plenty of light and solar gain from many large windows. The main feature is a double height living room with a beamed vaulted roof. Our bedroom was on the ground floor with two additional dormer-windowed bedrooms in the roof space, all with en suites.

The negotiations took many months and it was to be a year before builders had been contracted and the condemned cottage had been demolished.

We were able to afford this move because, out of the blue, an offer had been received to acquire the aquarium my company was running in Hastings. My partner and I, and the other shareholders, were not thinking of selling, but it was an offer it would have been foolish to refuse. How often is one likely to be approached by a person whose dearest wish is to buy an aquarium? The purchase included the smuggling exhibition and the 1066 experience at the castle as they were all part of a successful tourism package. The deal had been concluded in September the previous year.

*

Around that time, we received a letter from Isabella with another set-back. The Registry Office had received the document we had all signed guaranteeing that our house had been built to live in, not to sell; but now, nine months later, they were still refusing to register our house. This was on the grounds that we did not obtain a ten-year insurance warranty - whatever that might be - on completion of the building in December 2004. That was five years ago when nobody was clear what the hell was going on and the need for this guarantee was never mentioned. This meant that we did not, after all, officially own our house. Isabella had lodged an appeal.

2009 NOVEMBER - Spain for four weeks
Amazing progress! The old brick store had been replaced by a smart new *trastero* and at the other side of the house, exquisite terraces on two levels had appeared. Rafael had also created a shaded area on the upper terrace with walls and a pillar supporting a substantial roof. Luciana had provided the *ayuntamiento* with a completion certificate for the new *deposito* and rebuilt *trastero*, so the "store" could now be fitted with a shower-room.

There had recently been some heavy rain and the final fifty metres or so of the track up to our house had a deep gulley running down one side. The 4x4 only just made it, driving at a crazy angle. We discussed with Antonio the possibility of laying a concrete surface and, surprisingly, he volunteered to undertake the work himself. To mix and lay tons of concrete with steel reinforcement on a steep incline with no machinery apart from a battered old cement mixer, seemed an impossible task, but he dismissed our concerns saying that one of the neighbours would give him a hand. If we paid for the materials, both he and the neighbour were willing to contribute their labour as we would all benefit.

213

Josefina invited us for lunch one Sunday. The thought of conversing for another two hours was daunting but Alison's Spanish was gradually improving and they seemed to accept me as a hopeless case. Although the house had a kitchen with calor gas cooker, Josefina preferred to cook outside most of the year on a very smart brick barbecue with a tiled roof and chimney. A fire was lit and all kinds of meat and chopped vegetables were heaped into a large black pan. The smell was delicious, as was the food when cooked. On the table was fresh bread from the bread oven and wine from their own grapes. The wine, poured from a plastic lemonade bottle, was a light red colour, almost a rosé, with a dry slightly sharp taste that became palatable when one got used to it - by which time, one really did not care.

HOUSE WITH TERRACES

216

THE TRASTERO

Upper level frontage

Upper level room

Lower level room

Upper level en suite

HOUSE WITH TERRACES

Josefina cooking

Lunch with the neighbours

Burtie standing on neighbour's dog

Extraordinary cloud formations called 'Lenies' over our mountains

A week later, we plucked up courage to invite them to our house for a typically British Sunday lunch. The roast lamb was not as tasty as we had hoped as the meat from the market is not prepared as we are used to in England. However, the roast potatoes, a novelty, went down well. The bread and butter pudding was a great puzzle to them.

This was the time of year for picking olives. For the past few weeks our neigbours had both been working eight or ten-hour days harvesting olives from the scores of trees they owned and, by agreement, the olives on our land. This

was a laborious exercise that first involved clearing the entire area of weeds. It was then a matter of scrabbling around in the dirt to clear the fallen olives before spreading a large net under each tree in turn and shaking every branch to dislodge the fruit. Higher branches were lashed with a stout stick and combed with a big plastic rake. To make sure that nothing was missed, Antonio clambered up into the tree to dislodge anything still hanging on. The result was a pile of plastic crates brimming with *aceitunas* (olives) to be transported to the *molino* for pressing.

For a couple in their seventies, this seemed excessively tough work to produce only enough oil for their own use. With a good harvest, we were told, there might be a few bottles left over for relatives.

I made the mistake of trying to eat a black olive from one of our trees, and was forced to spit it out immediately. It was foul. Even after drinking quantities of water, this incredibly bitter taste persisted for a very long time. Apparently, olives have to go through a lot of processing before they are fit to eat. Well, you live and learn!

Josefina suggested we might like to accompany them to the *molino* (which translates as "mill" but, in this case is an oil press) to see their - and our - olives turned into oil. So, one morning we set out, following Antonio's van and trailer crammed full with crates full of olives. The journey, high up into the hills the other side of the valley, took nearly an hour. When we arrived at the *molino* around midday, there were quite a few farmers lined up waiting their turn. It would be some time before our olives could be unloaded, so we spent a fascinating half hour watching the process of squeezing the raw fruit into glistening oil.

First the sacks and crates were tipped through a grating into a pit where they were weighed so that the *molinero* (miller) knew how much to charge each customer. Antonio explained that this was why he had previously spread his olives out on the ground and left them for a few days to dry, before removing the leaves and twigs. This way, they were as light as possible. The weight having been recorded and agreed, a conveyor belt transported the olives over a grid allowing the fruit to fall through while the leaves, bits of bark and other detritus were deposited into a container at the end. Another elevator took the olives up to a higher level where they fell into a tank of water. From here they were transported on a wire belt - to get rid of excess moisture - before being dropped into a large trough with spiral mixing blades to grind and crush them into a paste. During this process, which takes around 45 minutes, small droplets of oil combine into bigger droplets.

Finally, the mixture was tipped into a centrifuge to separate the oil from the paste with the 'Extra Virgin' oil passing through a filter and pouring into the final tank. What remains after filtering can be further processed by running the centrifuge at a faster speed to produce a lower grade oil. Originally, the work of the centrifuge was carried out by a press, hence the terms "first pressing" and "second pressing".

Nothing is wasted. Even the pulp remaining after extracting the oil is deposited into a container to be collected by the farmer for animal fodder.

It was just as well we had our own car because Antonio and Josefina had to wait some hours before their olives were finally processed. It was dark when we heard them return.

The grating - on the right - where the sack of olives are poured to be weighed.

Conveyor belt taking olives up to be cleaned and crushed.

Spiral blades that will turn the olives into a paste.

Extra Virgin olive oil

CHAPTER THIRTY-FIVE
Water, Sewage And A Dead Horse

2010 APRIL - Spain for four weeks

Francisco had installed the pipe from our *deposito* down to the stopcock at the bottom of our land, but it needed a *regador* (a water man from the *comunidad de regantes*) to oversee the connection. So we were still reliant on water from Antonio.

Because of another winter with an unusual amount of rain, Antonio had not built the new concrete road and the track was in an even poorer state than when we left. He promised to have it completed before our next visit.

Seven months had passed since Isabella submitted her appeal regarding the non-registration of our house and she had only recently heard that it had now been "referred to a higher authority". That should take some time then!

The motorway was now open and our valley is no longer as quiet as it was, but the traffic noise was nowhere near as bad as we had feared. The tiny vehicles speeding along in the distance on the strip of concrete perched on top of impossibly high stilts, adds a point of interest when lazing on the terrace.

We were doing just that one afternoon, when we had an extraordinary and rather upsetting experience. The family on a neighbouring *finca* owned several fine horses, which they schooled in dressage and rode out over the hills most evenings. On this particular afternoon, a beautiful white horse was standing by a wire fence at the bottom of their land. On the other side of the fence there was a drop of about two metres down to the road. Alison noticed that the  horse seemed to be swaying from side to side and was just remarking on this strange behaviour when the poor thing fell through the fence and crashed down on to the road, ending up on its back, completely still.

One of the owners was working way above on his land and Alison ran up to alert him. We did not know if the horse was alive or dead so, not wanting to say the wrong thing, she said: "Your horse is ill. He is in the road." The man did not seem particularly surprised by this news.

"Yes, he is very old and ill."

The man came to have a look and verified that the animal was indeed dead.

As he was standing there, a builders merchant's lorry came along the track, heading back to Almuñécar. There was no way of getting past this large heavy carcase as it was completely blocking the road. We wondered what would happen next. By an extraordinary stroke of luck, it was one of those lorries that delivers pallets and large bags of sand and came equipped with a useful crane. Within a few minutes, the horse's hooves had been tied together and the crane had lifted the carcase into the air. The neighbour then fetched his 4x4 and the animal was lowered into the attached trailer and driven on to the neighbour's land. The lorry continued on its way. The brief drama ended as suddenly as it had begun. Everything was back to normal - except for the fact that a large and beautiful animal had just dropped dead before our eyes. In silence, we headed for the kitchen and put on the kettle.

A problem manifested itself with our very expensive septic tank. Once again, we were lazing on the lower terrace reading our books when our nostrils were assaulted by a pungent odour wafting up from below. Upon investigation, it became evident that our modern and expensive device with all its filters, tubes and tanks, was giving off a ripe old stench. This, despite Alison assiduously feeding the wretched thing on a regular basis with what we called "poo beetles", the sachets of special powder containing micro-organisms that had been so effective at *La Caracola*.

Our hi-tech system had only been used for a matter of months, but already it needed pumping out - something we never had to do with Eddie's concrete Poo Hut - and the operation was going to cost 375 euros - equal to more than £250 at the time.

The big tanker, bristling with pipes and hoses, arrived in the *rio seco* and we guided it up to our house. The young driver was apprehensive about manoeuvering this juggernaut up such a steep and narrow track. On several occasions he stopped to see how the vehicle was going to negotiate a tricky corner without toppling into the abyss. He was not a happy man.

Eventually we arrived and he began to unhitch sections of flexible pipe and fix them together to form a single pipe long enough to reach the septic tank. To our surprise, he was assisted by a very pretty young woman, obviously a novice in the sewage extraction business, as she had to be instructed how to handle each item of smelly pipe and connector as it came off the vehicle. We assumed that this was the girlfriend who had come along for a pleasant afternoon in the hills.

2010 NOVEMBER - Spain for five weeks

Antonio had constructed a splendid new concrete road. Now, even when the rains were washing the roads away elsewhere, there would be no problem driving up to our house. The neighbour failed to assist as promised, so Antonio had built the entire thing on his own. How a 73-year-old man with just a small cement mixer could achieve all this, we could not imagine.

Up at the house, no hot water. We contacted Urena and an engineer arrived later that day to look at the boiler. It did not take him long to discover that a mouse had eaten through all the electrical cables for the starting mechanism. With some spare lighting flex that I happened to have in the house, the problem was soon fixed. The engineer charged just 20 euros for his trouble.

Fed up with waiting for Francisco to contact the *regador* and organise the connection of our water pipe to the stopcock at the bottom of our land, Alison took the matter into her own hands. She rang up the *regador*, booked a time for him to do this work, then informed Francisco when he would be required.

When the day came, Antonio joined Francisco and the *regador* as they made the connection. The stopcock was opened. Nothing happened. There seemed to be a problem. A great deal of discussion and gesticulating ensued resulting in the *regador* turning on the second stopcock in the chamber. Gurgling noises were heard in the pipe and we all raced up the hill to our *deposito* where serious amounts of water were gushing in. Success! At last, we had our own water supply.

The euphoria was short-lived, however. The *regador* returned the next day and disconnected the pipe. Apparently, turning on the second stopcock was also sending water into a neighbour's deposito. He had spoken to *el presidente* at the *comunidad de regantes* office who said that the pipe was not owned by the *regantes,* it was privately installed and should not be used by us. There was nothing more he could do. So saying, he left.

This was reported to Antonio and we suggested, once again, that Rafael should make a permanent connection into the supply pipe to his *deposito;* but he was less than enthusiastic, finally admitting that he did not want the *regador* messing about on his property every time we needed water.

The chances of obtaining our own water supply seemed to have reached an impasse.

Meanwhile, distressing news from Isabella regarding the registration of the house. Her appeal has been turned down because we are claiming that there are two owners of the plot of land, which according to the Registrar, is impossible. They have no rules or guidelines for joint ownership so, as far as they are concerned, there is only one owner and one registered house - Antonio's. Even if this were not the case, our house could not be registered because we do not have the 10-year warranty.

Isabella took this judgement to the *notorio* who advised that we should do nothing until 2015 when the 10-year warrantee would run out and the Registrar would then have no grounds for not registering the house. At that point, Isabella would be in a strong position to negotiate legal separation of the land in accordance with our private agreement. If the Registrar still argued that there was no precedent for segregating such a small piece of land, then he suggested that the two houses might be registered as a block of flats each owned separately. Either that, or register the plot as a very small housing estate.

This was a far from unsatisfactory situation, and a worrying uncertainty we would have to live with for the next four to five years.

CHAPTER THIRTY-SIX
A Lucky Chance Meeting

2011 MARCH - Spain for five weeks

Our water supply was still coming down a hosepipe from Antonio's deposito and looked like remaining that way. It remained a mystery why the stopcock at the bottom of our land, used by Antonio for many years, could possibly belong to someone else. Antonio was equally puzzled and agreed to accompany us to the office of the *comunidad de regantes* to argue our case.

Antonio insisted on talking to *el presidente* himself and the two of them discussed the problem at length before plans were produced showing all the water pipes in our area. Apparently this proved that the only supply we could possibly tap into was the one leading down into Antonio's *deposito*. It was never explained to us why this should be but, for some reason, Antonio was persuaded and the meeting came to a conclusion.

Somewhat depressed, we left the office and headed for the nearest café/bar where an elderly gentleman seated at one of the tables, waved at Antonio and beckoned us over. We were introduced to Joaquin, the owner of a *finca* that was right opposite our electricity pole a quarter of a mile from our land. Joaquin, a well-upholstered figure with the ruddy complexion and droopy eyes of a man who enjoyed his alcohol, was drinking a large brandy. Coffees were ordered for the rest of us while Antonio explained about our meeting at the *comunidad de regantes;* water being a constant topic of interest in the *campo* As the two men chatted, the conversation became more serious and they seemed to be arriving at an agreement about something. There was a pause. Joaquin nodded at Antonio as if to say "Go ahead" and, turning to us, Antonio announced the good news.

We had been told by the *comunidad de regantes* that we could not use the stopcock on our land that had briefly provided us with water because it was also connected to a "private" pipe. Amazingly, Joaquin had just revealed that he was the owner of this pipe. Furthermore, as he had recently built himself a large *deposito* supplied from a different pipe, he had no use for this old water connection. For a price to be agreed, he would be willing to give us the right to one hour of water when required.

We were invited to his house for coffee the following day to agree terms. Antonio came along to see fair play and Josefina, a great friend of Joaquin's wife Anna, joined the party. Their house of 50m^2, plus porches and terraces, was a variation of the standard size allowed in the *campo*. Like most owners, they used it mainly at weekends, only visiting the *finca* to tend to crops and feed the assortment of dogs. During the week, Joaquin and Anna lived in a much larger detached house on the outskirts of Almuñécar.

Coffees were served and after an hour of general chatter to which we were unable to contribute, Joaquin indicated that it was time to get down to business. Josefina and Anna retired to the kitchen and Alison was obviously meant to follow. Discussions about water and money were men's business. Although perfectly aware of what was expected, she firmly took her place with Antonio, Joaquin and me sitting around the dining table. Joaquin found it difficult to look her in the eye whenever she asked a question and always referred his answers to me, although it was obvious that Alison had a much better grasp of what was being said.

Having no idea what sort of money Joaquin had in mind for the use of his pipe, there was a stunned silence when a figure of 3,000 euros was mentioned. True, he had paid for the pipework some years ago, probably not very much, but he now had no use for it. Moreover, there were no further costs involves as we would be paying for water directly to the *comunidad*. All he was actually selling was the right to use his old pipe.

Alison asked Antonio if she had heard correctly and he, looking slightly uncomfortable, confirmed that this was indeed the figure.

Joaquin thought he had us over a barrel. A good water supply in the hills was like gold dust, but this was an excessive amount. Alison and I had a quick conversation and decided to call his bluff and decline the offer unless he could accept a figure of 1,500 euros, explaining that our new *deposito* had cost so much that we simply did not have the money. If this was unacceptable, we still had an entitlement for water from Antonio. Of course, 1,500 euros was still a complete rip-off but this was our only opportunity of making *El Escondrijo* entirely self-sufficient.

In her best Spanish, Alison put forward our proposal, but Joaquin, being one of those men who found it difficult to discuss money with a woman, failed to grasp what she was saying. It was left to Antonio to explain our offer.

Joaquin reacted as though he could not believe our nerve in suggesting such a derisory figure, indicating in no uncertain terms that he found it an insult.

There was an awkward silence. We had nothing further to say and Joaquin was obviously not going to budge.

Antonio stood up, touched Joaquin on the arm and indicated that they should have a private conversation. The two men removed themselves into the kitchen, just out of earshot. We hoped that Antonio was pointing out that we were the only people who could possibly be interested in his pipe, saying something along the lines that our offer was a very fair deal, certainly more than any Spanish person would pay. Surely, 1,500 euros had to be better than no euros at all.

At the conclusion of this muttered conversation, they returned to the table and Antonio informed us that Joaquin now understood our financial situation and had generously offered to halve the price.

We could hardly believe it. Thanks to Antonio, we had our water. The relief of tension in the room was palpable. The next problem was how and when to pay. There was insufficient cash in our Spanish account and, until our Welsh farmhouse was sold, money was extremely tight at home. So Alison tentatively proposed in Spanish that we should pay 500 euros now and…

She got no further. As soon as Joaquin heard the words "500 euros", he exploded, angrily shouting that 500 euros was ridiculous and the deal was off. Once again, Antonio calmed things down by quietly suggesting that Alison should be allowed to finish what she was saying. She continued:

"…and then, next April when we come back to Spain, we can give you another 1,000 euros. We do not have 1,500 euros in Spain."

Antonio chipped in to vouch for our honesty. He said that we were good *amigos* and he was sure that and the money would be paid in April.

This took a moment to sink in. Then Joaquin muttered an unenthusiastic "Si."

"Si?" enquired Alison, not sure that he was agreeing.

"Si." He replied. This time more definitely.

Alison looked at me. I look at Antonio. He was smiling. It was a deal. We shook hands with Joaquin and then Alison spoke again in her best Spanish.

"We have a contract, yes? We all go to *el presidente de la comunidad de regantes* and sign a paper, yes?"

Joaquin shrugged, indicating that this was not necessary, but agreed to meet us the following morning at the *comunidad* office.

We assumed that there would be some sort of standard contract but we wanted to ensure that a few vital points were covered; most importantly, that we would have rights to the water in perpetuity. As a check-list, that evening we created our own very simple draft contract and translated it into Spanish.

At the meeting with *el presidente*, he and Joaquin chatted for some time before we were asked to verify our names and show our passports. A secretary then recorded the details of the arrangement in a book and *el presidente* declared that all was satisfactory and we could now make the connection.

Alison offered our thanks, but suggested that everybody should sign a paper so that we all had a record of the agreement. *El Presidente* seemed puzzled. This was obviously not the way things were normally done. He looked up enquiringly at Joaquin who merely shrugged, indicating that it was a matter of indifference to him. Nobody seemed to know how to proceed, so Alison produced our piece of paper, written in her best 'O' level Spanish, and laid it on the desk. We had made an extra copy for Joaquin to read and one for us.

There had been no discussion about any financial transaction and when *el presidente* saw the figure of 1,500 euros, his eyebrows shot up and he only just stopped himself from making a comment. Instead, he gave Joaquin a quizzical look, but Joaquin quickly looked away pretending to be studying a poster on the wall.

Everybody seemed happy to sign our document and *el presidente* confirmed that we now had the right to fill up our 60,000 litre *deposito* once a week at the cost of 16 euros each time (although, realistically, we would only need four or five refills a year). In addition, there was an annual standing charge of 38 euros. These very modest prices were to rise substantially during the forthcoming years.

The ceremony was concluded with the handing over of an envelope containing the first payment of 500 euros to Joaquin, and we all parted company on good terms.

El Escondrijo had its own water supply and we were entirely self-sufficient at last.

2012 APRIL/MAY - Spain for five weeks

On our first weekend, we strolled round to Joaquin's house and paid the 1,000 euros owed. He signed a receipt for the money and we all agreed that the deal was now complete and everyone was happy.

The deposito was nearly empty, so for the first time, we ordered our own water. This turned out to be a complicated business. First, one had to be issued with a book of water tickets at the *comunidad de regantes* office. Then, after filling out a ticket, one had to visit the *comunidad's* bank - with the inevitable long wait - to make a payment. This you could only do on two mornings a week between 9.00 a.m. and 11.00 a.m. but not at all during the last week of the month. The tickets were in three parts: one for us, one to be retained by the bank, and one to be taken back to the *comunidad's* office and placed in a box for collection by the *regador*. The following day we had to telephone the *regador* to say that we were waiting for water. Normally, he would turn up within a day or two to operate the stopcock.

With plenty of water now available, we began to wonder about an irrigation system. Perhaps we could have colourful flowers and shrubs around the house where there were currently just cacti and a few plants in pots that Antonio and Josephina kindly kept watered. And it would be wonderful to grow climbers around our stark chicken-wire security fence.

The *fincas* all have irrigation systems to water their olive and fruit trees and other crops. Black *goma* (hosepipe) is laid on the ground around the trees with *goteros* (dribblers) that leak water whenever the main tap is turned on. This is usually once a day for half an hour or so.

We asked Antonio if this was a job that Francisco could undertake, but were told that this was not possible - and the explanation really shook us. Only a month or so previously Francisco had been building a *deposito* for a farmer high up in a remote area and when he did not return home after a couple of days, a search party was sent out. His body was found near where he had been working.

From the evidence, it looked likely that his car - perhaps with the brake not properly on - had started rolling backwards down the track. Francisco had tried to get into the car to stop it but the tyre marks showed where he and the vehicle had left the track and crashed down into the valley. Badly injured, he had tried to climb back up to the road. He had not made it.

Our splendid *deposito* always reminds us of this endearingly jovial character and his terribly sad end.

Regarding the irrigation system, Antonio suggested that we could organize this ourselves and directed us to a specialist shop where they recommended an automatic watering system comprising a timer and a small electric pump. Two days later a man arrived to construct a small brick *casita* to house the pump and the following evening, when the cement was dry, the equipment was installed.

Antonio came by as I was laying the *goma* and watched, amused, as I struggled to insert the little *goteros*. Making a hole with the special tool provided was not a problem, but it required a great deal of force to push the little blighters in. Of course, he offered to help - which meant actually doing all the work while I tried to assist by handing him things - not always what he wanted. It was galling to see how quickly and easily he used his thumb to press in the *goteros*. But then, he was immensely strong and this was something he had been doing for years. His own land must have hundreds of these little dribblers.

An hour or so later, we had *goma* running around the top two terraces of our land providing water for an avocado, a lemon, two orange trees and the 'garden'. While we were at it, Antonio and I decided to include the eight olive trees on these terraces. Since purchasing the property, the trees had become sadder and sadder and we hated to see them producing mean little *aceitunas* through lack of water.

Job done, we were looking forward to being able to pick our own avocados, oranges and lemons from the revitalised trees. We felt it better to leave the collection of our olives to our neighbours who, quite unnecessarily, presented us with a large plastic bottle of delicious olive oil every year.

Apart from her rabbits, chickens and ducks, Josefina also kept two nanny goats. They were high maintenance, as two hours had to be set aside every evening for walking them over the hills to find food, but the milk they gave was all part of our neighbours' self sufficient life-style. One of the goats, having spent some time at a neighbouring *finca* where they had a billy, had produced two kids. Now about two months old, we were invited to see them. For a person brought up in the country with animals, Josefina was surprisingly affectionate with her babies, giving them lots of cuddles and kisses. But they were extremely cute.

One Sunday, Antonio and Josefina had a big family get-together and we were invited to lunch along with various brothers, sisters and in-laws. Josefina and one of her sisters were busy at the barbecue tending a saucepan full of vegetables and an enormous pan overflowing with meat. Several months had passed since we had been introduced to the baby goats and we feared the worst. There was no avoiding the issue. We were about to eat one of them. All we had to do was treat this as just another piece of meat and try to forget the image of the little creature licking our hands and staring at us with those big trusting eyes.

2012 JUNE - Forest of Dean

During our previous trip to Spain in April, builders had laid the foundations for the new house in the Forest of Dean. I had thought that we would be there to oversee the process as the work had been scheduled for completion before we went away. Upon our return, we were not pleased to see the concrete pad a few feet further from the road than shown on the drawing, resulting in a larger front garden and smaller back garden than planned. Worse was to come, but only became evident some months later when the internal walls started going up. The foundations were a foot (30cm) short in both directions resulting in the central wall of the house being about eight inches (20cm) out of place. The builder tried to blame my drawings and we were forced to pay for a Quantity Surveyor to arbitrate. Fortunately, he agreed that my plans were perfectly adequate and his intervention resulted in several minor walls being knocked down and rebuilt.

By June, ten months later than promised, the new house was ready for occupation. Tal-y-Fan Farm had finally been sold and we said a sad farewell to our home on the Welsh hill.

At the new house, the exterior work of building walls and terraces had been removed from the builder's contract and we asked Wilf, our wonderful Welsh builder, if he could take on this work. He was appalled at the standard of work in the house and although it meant a journey of well over an hour each way, he and his son Ross came to our rescue. It was such a relief to have pleasant people on site who actually took a pride in their work.

THIRTY-SEVEN
The Final Chapter

Visiting *El Escondrijo* each year in Spring and Autumn has become a regular feature in our lives. The house now works perfectly. Switch on the electricity, light the gas water heater and we are in business. It takes less than two hours to clean the house, make the bed and unpack the clothes we keep there.

A typical day will involve a trip to the market in Almuñécar to buy locally grown fruit and vegetables and fresh fish, then on to one of the small supermarkets for other provisions such as milk, juice and water. There always has to be a break for coffee at a cafe run by a lady called Lola with her two sons. Dogs are officially not permitted but the first time we poked our heads in the door, she saw Burtie and waved us in. There is only room for around thirty people and it is usually packed with regulars, a great number of whom are middle-aged or elderly women. The place is a riot of chatter and laughter with Lola and her sons joining in the banter. The coffee is the best in the world, especially when accompanied by a warm *ensaimada*, a small pastry in a flat coil shape, deliciously soft and buttery, sprinkled with icing sugar. Burtie sits under the table and appears to enjoy the atmosphere as much as we do.

On some days we go down to the town early to take breakfast at Lola's. This is always coffee with *tostada* (half a small toasted loaf) upon which you pour olive oil before adding a smear of pureed tomato and salt. Wonderful.

The rest of the day might be spent pottering in the garden, doing little painting jobs around the house, or reading, resting, eating and drinking in the sunshine. Inevitably, Alison will be writing or planning her next one-woman show, or possibly making costumes or props. As the full company is on tap, the producer (Alison), the author (Alison), the cast (Alison) and the director (me), we have even been known to take advantage of the peace and quiet to hold rehearsals. So far, *El Escondrijo* has seen the birth of three new plays.

The garden is maturing. Now we have the water supply, many of the cacti have been replaced with flowering shrubs. The avocado and lemon trees

237

always have an abundance of fruit and Antonio has planted several more trees for us including two mangos, a fig and a "better" orange, plus a couple of grape vines. It is obvious that bringing the land he once owned back to life gives him pleasure, but we were feeling guilty that he was doing so much for us and wondered if he might accept some payment. Concerned that he might be offended, we tentatively suggested a small sum of money every six months as compensation for his time. What did he think? Would this be acceptable? *"Si"*, he said as though we had offered him a cup of coffee, and the matter was discussed no further. The money is given and received without any embarrassment.

A few cosmetic improvements have been made to the house. Rafael has added an edging of tiles around our flat roof, built a porch for the front door and installed a wrought gate in the security fence, now almost covered with greenery. The lower storeroom of the *trastero* has become a useful workroom or spare bedroom with an additional window and a smart new door, and a new store has been constructed on the far side of the *deposito* to house all the garden tools, paints and other bric-a-brac.

Rafael adding decorative roof tiles

Josefina often drops by with gifts of fruit, eggs or something particularly Spanish she has just baked. In return Alison will make sponge cakes or macaroons, a novelty particularly welcomed by Antonio. On one occasion, she made them a batch of éclairs, only they were not as successful as she had hoped. The Spanish chocolate was not great and the Spanish cream looked and tasted like Crazy Foam. Antonio, of course, ate them with enthusiasm. The next day we were presented with an olive oil flavoured loaf fresh from Josefina's bread oven and a plastic box full of home-grown peanuts and almonds also roasted in the bread oven. Together with some olives, slithers of *jamon Serrano* and avocados from our own tree, it was a delicious feast.

Our expensive and complicated sewage system began to smell again. If it was going to cost around £250 to have it emptied every other year, perhaps we should consider replacing it with something that worked. However, the man who came up to clear the tank for the second time, said that it was not actually full. The odour was coming from an exhaust pipe on top of the unit. This was normal with these modern units. The simple answer was to fit a flexible plastic pipe to the exhaust and run it along the ground as far away from the house as possible. Problem solved. The bill came to 204 euros.

The year 2015 was ten years from the official completion of the building, so the period of the ten-year warranty that we never obtained had now elapsed. This meant that there was no longer any reason to withhold registration of our house. It was time for Isabella to visit the registrar to discuss both the registration and the legal separation of our land.

The result of the meeting was that the Registrar was still refusing to segregate the plot. It must remain as one parcel of land. The *notorio's* alternative ideas of the land being registered as a mini housing estate or the two houses treated as a block of flats were rejected out of hand. So the only record of who owns which piece of the plot of land is the original private agreement.

The good news was that, at last, the house has been officially registered in our name. The ownership cannot be challenged - with the proviso, as Isabella pointed out, that all land in Spain is owned by the Crown.

"Should it be deemed necessary to, say, build a motorway through your property, there is little one can do about it. Fortunately, on your particular hill, the chances of that happening are not very likely, mm?"

I said that, after all the agony we had been through to establish the right to live in our own house, it would be a typical end to the whole experience to have it bulldozed to make way for a motorway.

"I agree that you have been particularly unfortunate, but I do not think you need to worry about that."

"But why on earth were we given such a hard time? Is it just us?"

"No, it is not you. Other people were suffering too, and the reason has now become clear. It was bad timing. There has recently been a lot of discussion in the newspapers about a ridiculous local law that was introduced all those years ago when we first tried to register your property. Apparently, Manuel Chaves, President of the Junta de Andalucia was flying over the countryside in his helicopter one day and noticed that more and more houses were springing up everywhere. What was going on? The countryside was being ruined. He was told that it was all the foreigners flocking to Spain to buy up cheap plots of land for their holiday homes. Just like you, mm?

So he decided this had to stop. With no warning, on the 31ˢᵗ December 2003, when everyone was on holiday, he brought in this new law. No permission to be given for new homes in the countryside. The town planners, with so many projects in the pipeline, were thrown into confusion, and they have still been given no proper guidance on how to proceed. It is our bad luck to be caught up in this fiasco."

So that was the answer. It was merely some stupid local piece of legislation that had given us all those years of heartache. Fortunately, we had persevered and despite the machinations of our friend, the Annoying Little Git and his accomplices - who we now know were operating under impossible constraints - we had won through. Somewhere in the *ayuntamineto* there is definitely a file stating that we are the official owners of El Escondrijo.

*

By the time our house was finally registered, it was getting on for thirty years since our friends Tony and Monique had first lent us their house in Los Tablones and set us on this extraordinary adventure.

So, after all we have been through, was it worth it? For us, the answer is a resounding yes. We loved *La Caracola*, our first little cottage, and *El Escondrijo*, once built, has been a constant joy. We are constantly amazed at the view and we are always grateful for the additional ten weeks or so of sunshine we enjoy each year. It has been a journey full of highs and - rather too many - lows, but as time passes the memories of the dark days seem insignificant when contemplating what we have achieved.

Would we recommend others to embark upon a similar enterprise? Well, if you have the desire and the ability to design your own home, are blessed with a certain amount of tenacity, and also happen to be barking mad, why not?

Do we have any advice? Absolutely. Before contemplating the purchase of a ruin or a plot, it is vital to seek legal advice to ensure that the vendor has the right to sell. You must also ascertain that there are no building restrictions and that the property has both water and electricity. Then, it is absolutely essential for all the paperwork and transfer of money to be handled by your lawyer. Finally, it is crucial to find a builder who comes with personal recommendations.

But then, we did all that, didn't we?

EL ESCONDRIJO - 2016

Postscript

By 2015, both Antonio and I were in our late seventies and he was wondering how much longer he and Josefina could continue the arduous work involved in the upkeep of their land. Similarly, we were thinking it might be time to move somewhere that did not involve water pumps, gas bottles, septic tanks and driving up riverbeds. We all agreed that it was time to sell.

Because the two properties could not be legally separated, we agreed that the entire plot with both houses should be placed on the market. Possibly someone might wish to live in one of the houses and keep the other for holiday lets. Not one of the agents we approached was happy about this arrangement. People tend to search on websites in price brackets and, for the amount we were asking, they would expect to find villas by the sea with gardens and swimming pools.

Unfortunately, they were right. Although we were on the books of five agents, a year later there had not been a single enquiry.

Then someone suggested that we approach another agent in Almuñecar who actually lived in the *campo* and had a reputation for selling country properties. This was to lead to an extraordinary revelation.

Carlos did not speak much English but we were able to explain the details of our situation to his wife who was Irish. We showed them a plan of the entire plot and the official survey of our portion of the land. He took these to his computer and looked up the *catastral* plan produced by the Land Registry Office.

"This is not correct. The survey of your land shows an extra piece of land below the road, but this is not coloured green on the *catastral* plan. Do you own that extra piece of land?"

"Yes. Absolutely."

"Then the *catastral* plan is wrong. Do you have a copy of your *escritura*?"

We had brought along all the paperwork and were able to produce the document. Unlike property deeds in the UK, an *escritura* does not incorporate a plan. The extent of the land is described in words by specifying square metres, roads, natural features and the borders of neighbours' land. The *catastral* plan was a separate item that Isabella had acquired much later when obtaining the *certificado de catastral* for the annual land tax.

Carlos pointed at a paragraph in the *escritura*.

"It says that your plot is "dry land" but the *catastral* plan says it is agricultural. Also, your official survey states that you own 2,588 metres of land. So your *escritura* appears to be wrong."

"What does that actually mean?"

"It means that if you have olive trees and irrigation, then it is definitely agricultural land. Dry land is no good. Legally, you need 2,500 metres of agricultural land to segregate. This you appear to have. You must talk to your *abogada*."

Later that day, we telephoned Isabella to report this bombshell. After all her unsuccessful endeavours over the past eleven years to segregate our properties, we expected her to be mortified to have missed such an error, or at least show some surprise. On the contrary, she merely replied:

"I will look into this for you. But you must realise it will mean having a new land survey, a new certificado de catastro, and drawing up a completely new *escritura* and *nota simple*. All this will take more than a year, of course. It is a pity that you did not noticed these anomalies before, mm?"

Incensed by this response, we sought a second opinion from an *abogado* recommended by Carlos. Unfortunately, he agreed with Isabella's assessment of the situation. So, we contacted our project architect, Luciana, and asked her to organise a land survey. She warned us that, ten years on, the survey would be more thorough and technically sophisticated than the original; consequently much more expensive. Of course.

The survey confirmed that we own 2,656 square meters. This includes the rough road at the bottom of our property that Antonio says is our land. However, in case the Registrar insists on discounting the road, we asked how much land would remain. It looked to us that we still might not have the required 2,500 square meters. The surveyor came back with a figure of 2,500.9 square meters! This is now official. Let the Registrar try to argue with that.

Our *certificado de catastro* has now been updated. The next step is for Isabella to obtain a licence of segregation. Then the *notario* has to write to the owners of land abutting our borders to inform them of the changes. Finally, it is a matter of revising the *escritura* and *nota simple* to prove that we really are sole owners of both house and land.

The estate agents all agree that selling the two properties separately without legal complications will be much easier. When sold, our plan is to find a little house near the town that has mains water and electricity, and is approached by a tarmac road; preferably, an older property that has potential for a modest but carefully designed *reforma*. There are bound to be some hiccoughs along the way, but that is of no concern to us.

This time we know what we are doing…

About the author

DAVID COLLISON began his career as an assistant stage manager at the Arts Theatre Club in London. He went on to become a renowned sound designer and during the 1970s and 80s, worked on more than fifty West End musicals including *Fiddler on the Roof, Cabaret, Sweet Charity, A Funny Thing Happened on the Way to the Forum, Mame, A Little Night Music, Grease, Company, Applause, Joseph and the Technicolor Dreamcoat* and *Jesus Christ Superstar.*

He was Sound Designer for the Royal Shakespeare Company under Sir Peter Hall and for the National Theatre Company under Sir Laurence Olivier. As a sound consultant, he designed permanent sound systems for theatres and concert halls in the UK and around the world, including the National Theatre of Great Britain.

David was privileged to work with many illustrious performers including Bing Crosby, Julie Andrews, Sammy Davis Jnr., Judi Dench, Kenneth Williams, Maggie Smith, Michael Crawford, Leslie Caron, Ginger Rogers, Elizabeth Taylor, John Mills, Peter Sellers, Bruce Forsyth, Sean Connery, Harry Secombe, Tommy Steele, Max Bygraves, Lauren Bacall, Johnny Matthis, Jean Simmons, Peter Cook and Dudley Moore, the whole of the Dad's Army Team and many more.

In 1988 he formed Adventure Projects to use his theatrical talents for the creation of themed visitor attractions, two of which received English Tourist Board Awards for Excellence. In 2007, David Collison received the USITT Harold Burris-Meyer Distinguished Career in Sound Design Award. In 2013, he was made an Honorary Fellow of the Royal Central School for Speech and Drama.

He has written two acclaimed books on theatre sound (*Stage Sound* and *The Sound of Theatre*), a play for children adapted from Hans Andersen's *The Tinder Box*, plus numerous scripts for audio-visuals and videos.

soundoftheatre.com

"The whole book is such an informative record of its subject."

HAL PRINCE (Broadway producer)

"A fascinating journey through the development of sound from the Ancient Greeks to the basics of the technology we have today."

JAMES EADE (Lighting & Sound International)

"An absolutely captivating read. What a tour de force!"

DAVID E. SMITH (Director of sound - North Carolina School of Arts)

Dear reader,

If you have been at all amused by our story, it would be wonderful if you could mention it to your friends on social media. A pleasant review on Amazon would be even more appreciated.

Thank you.

To see YouTube of house:

https://youtu.be/HsJPABWVhHU

Printed in Poland
by Amazon Fulfillment
Poland Sp. z o.o., Wrocław